GO F*CK YOURSELF, CIAN!

I WOULD LIKE TO DEDICATE THIS BOOK TO A FEW THINGS. FIRSTLY I WOULD LIKE TO DEDICATE THIS BOOK TO MY TOILET SEAT, MY IPHONE AND MY COUCH. THESE THREE ITEMS ENABLED ME TO WRITE THIS ENTIRE BOOK.

SECONDLY I WOULD LIKE TO THANK MY MOTHER, LIZ, MY SISTER, REBECCA, AND THE REST OF MY FAMILY AND FRIENDS. YOU'VE ALL HELPED AND SUPPORTED ME EVEN THOUGH IT WAS REALLY FUCKING WEIRD TO ACT LIKE MY GIRLFRIEND AND MAKE INTERNET VIDEOS. I'M GLAD YOU'VE ALL ACCEPTED MY WEIRDNESS.

THIRDLY I WOULD LIKE TO DEDICATE THIS BOOK TO MY GIRLFRIEND, EMILY. WHEN YOU MET ME I WAS A BOY AND YOU'VE HELPED ME TURN INTO A MAN. THANK YOU FOR SUPPORTING EVERY DECISION I'VE EVER MADE AND THANK YOU FOR BEING THE OTHER HALF TO MY CAREER. I LOOK FORWARD TO MAKING MANY, MANY MORE WITH YOU.

LASTLY I NEED TO THANK MY PSYCHO ALTER EGO EMILY: SHE'S A FUCKING CRAZY LITTLE BITCH BUT WITHOUT HER I WOULD BE NOTHING. YOU'RE THE BEST, EMILY. THANKS FOR LIVING INSIDE MY HEAD.

Published by Blink Publishing
3.08, The Plaza,
535 Kings Road,
Chelsea Harbour,
London, SW10 0SZ

www.blinkpublishing.co.uk

facebook.com/blinkpublishing
twitter.com/blinkpublishing

Hardback – 978-1-911-2748-72
Ebook – 978-1-911-2749-71

A CIP catalogue of this book is available from the British Library.

Designed by Steve Leard
Printed and bound by UAB Balto

3 5 7 9 10 8 6 4 2

All images courtesy of Joseph Sinclair and Shutterstock, except pp. 11, 13, 23, 29, 35, 41, 46, 51, 75, 79, 83, 93, 125, 129, 130, 161, 166, 173, 195 © Cian Twomey, and p. 49 © Getty Images

Every reasonable effort has been made to trace copyright holders of material reproduced in this book, but if any have been inadvertently overlooked the publishers would be glad to hear from them.

Blink Publishing is an imprint of the Bonnier Publishing Group
www.bonnierpublishing.co.uk

THE WEIRD DUDE FROM FACEBOOK PRESENTS...

GO F*CK YOURSELF, CIAN!

MY MAD LIFE WITH MY INSANE OTHER HALF

CIAN TWOMEY

BLINK
bringing you closer

CONTENTS

PART 3 – MOVING IN

PART 4 – THE FUTURE

INTRODUCTION
BY CIAN TWOMEY

Hello, hi, hello, how are you keeping, how are you doing, that's good, that's very good, okay let's go.

So if you know who I am then I don't need to explain but if you're standing in the airport wondering who the fuck this fat little creep is on the front cover, my name is Cian and the other person, who is also me, is my alter ego, Emily. She's nice, not really. Horrible, in fact, but nonetheless a funny one: funny to laugh at, not with.

But anyway, here we go. Welcome to my book! It's kind of like a funny bible for people who have no fucking idea what they're doing in their relationship. Now I shit you not I am no way qualified to give you professional relationship advice, but I've been through enough shit with my girlfriend that I feel like a grand master and I've survived all of the impossible challenges. I've gathered all of my tips, tricks and ways to deal with a fucking maniac of a partner. Not a real maniac, but close.

You'll also see some inputs from my alter ego, Emily, in this book. She insisted that she wanted to be included, and threatened to kill a puppy if I were to not have her in this. So they sit alongside my anecdotal advice – from what to do when you have to mention your previous girlfriends for the first time, to how to finally 'pop' the question...

Also guys, just to say that my alter-ego Emily is a work of fiction and I in no way condone any of the weird advice she gives. She's just part of my weird imagination – so please don't practice any of what she preaches!

Enjoy it, try not to fall asleep or use this book as a chopping board for your onions. Just buy it actually; I couldn't give a shit what you do with it.

PREFACE
BY EMILY

Hello mothafuckas! You're gonna be seeing me a lot in this book so I feel like you're going to need my opinion or some shit about the book before you read it.

Considering I wrote all of it, I feel like it's pretty much the shittiest thing I've ever attempted so if you're looking for something to amuse you or even make you smirk then don't buy this book. In fact it does the opposite of making you smile, it's so fuckin' bad that it makes you want to go and jump off a fucking cliff sweet lord Jesus help me.

I'm just kidding by the way, this book is so good it can make you a millionaire. I promise, just have patience and the divorce settlement will land eventually. It's what I'm fucking banking on anyway. Thank God Cian likes to save his money. Anyway welcome to da fuckin' book, sexy ladies and sexy gentlemen!

Emily xxx

ANOTHER PREFACE
BY THE REAL EMILY

Hi guys, it's Emily here, no not psycho Emily, the real one…

Cian asked me to write a little paragraph for the book and well here I am. After two years of being Cian's girlfriend, I have learned a lot about being in a relationship. I have learned that you can eat takeaways every single weekend with the love of your life and can put on an few extra pounds but you're okay with that right?

Also in the past two years, Cian and myself have travelled the world, made amazing memories together and, of course, created some weird-ass content for your entertainment on Facebook/YouTube. Which, may I add, was the most fun out of everything! From writing scripts with Cian to being Cian's camera woman, it was all so much fun. I really hope some of the videos on Facebook/YouTube have made you smile and I hope that reading this book will also make you smile.

I love you all so much, thank you for taking your time to read what I have to say… Now go eat some chicken nuggets and enjoy the book.

Lots of love,
Emily Rochford

P.S. Just a cheeky little plug…
Follow me on Instagram:
@missemilyrochford

FOREWORD
BY CIAN'S MAM

Boy... didn't I do a good job? The one thing I can tell you about my son is that from a very young age I knew there was a comedian stuck inside him bursting to get out. He definitely got his humour from his father's side because from time to time he keeps telling me to lighten up.

Am I proud? Yes. Do I worry? Yes. But underneath the façade of humour there is a very sensible 22-year-old, which I like to call 'old man's ass'. From the time he met Emily the sparks were forming, the volcanos were erupting and the flowers were blooming. I knew from then it was love at first sight.

Before I could take a breath Emily was living in my house, *cough cough*

rent-free. She became like a daughter to me (stop whinging, Rebecca). And the house has become very quiet since they both moved out (apart from the usual rants coming from Becky). It saddened me when they left, but it filled my heart with happiness knowing that Cian's in very safe hands with Emily (knowing I would do a better job but that's the mammy coming out in me).

The one thing I know for sure is that Cian will always be there for me and will always be present in my life and I love both Cian and Emily with all my heart.

Cian – I am very proud of you and the man you have become today. Xx

PROLOGUE: CIAN'S WEIRD JOB LIVING WITH CIAN

If you don't know me, let me tell you about what I do. To put it simply, my professional career is to video myself arguing with my alter-ego girlfriend who is based on my real-life girlfriend. You got it? Cool.

So my real girlfriend, Emily, is asked hundreds of times a week 'what's it like living with Cian' and to be quite honest she's sick as fucking shit of having to answer that question so I'm just going to clear it all up and let you know exclusively how Emily feels about my job.

Emily is the most supporting and encouraging person I've ever met. When I'm stuck for video ideas or I'm not feeling motivated to be productive, she is constantly there to help me out and allows me to create great content for over 5 and a half million followers to enjoy.

She has had to get used to a few things first.

Camera: most couples leave their things carelessly scattered around the house such as underwear or socks. Me though? I leave a camera around every fucking square inch of my house. I can't help it, I get the habit of thinking that I need that fancy camera and end up not using them. I should really consider going and selling them so I can buy myself a pet llama. I can sense they'll be the trend soon.

When Emily is at home with me, I make my videos in front of her all the time. So sometimes she could be in the living room, enjoying a movie and having some popcorn. I would then storm in and tell her to mute the TV while I record a video. She sits in silence and watches me create really fucking weird videos that people seem to enjoy.

Recently I've brought Emily into the videos just to get her more involved. I'm delighted because she's showing huge interest and now she can be credited as she's literally 50 per cent of the video! Plus she's my talented cameraperson. Don't worry, she gets paid well for being my little assistant.

Emily also had to get over the fact that she could come home one day to find me dressed head to toe in her clothes. Now I know what you're thinking! 'Jeez, Cian is with Emily for now but down the line he mightn't be swinging in the same direction.'

Well, to be fair I can see your point, but if I'm totally honest I just find shit funny and putting a fat bearded Irish man in a floral dress is something Emily knows not to worry about, she understands that I just do it for dat YouTube monaaay.

One time Emily came home with her friend and they were greeted by me in the kitchen wearing bright red lipstick in a pink hoodie and my eyeshadow jet black like my soul. No one seems to question it any more, they're all just kinda like 'meh, yeah.. he's just our weird ole Cian.'

Overall, I think she's cool with it. Although it seems like it's all fun and games, Emily understands and respects that I treat this like any other professional business. Plus she gets fancy gifts occasionally, so she has no fucking reason to complain, lol.

PART 1
HOW IT STARTED

WHEN YOU MENTION PREVIOUS GIRLFRIENDS...

You see, whenever Emily asked me about previous girlfriends, I would try my best to steer the conversation in a totally different direction.

'What was your ex like?'

Oh shit. Okay do you prefer moths or butterflies? I personally like butterflies because Monarch butterflies are known for their long migration. Every year Monarch butterflies will travel a great distance (sometimes over 4,000 km), females will lay eggs and a new generation of Monarchs will travel back, completing the cycle and—

'CIAN?!'

'Oh, yeah what? Sorry, babe... what was the question?'

If you want to find out more about your partner's ex-lovers, prepare yourself for an answer you don't want to hear. It's dangerous territory because you're literally saying, 'Oh, what was the person who was here before me like?'

Even though I avoided the question at all costs because I don't want Emily getting all angered up because of my past, now I just tell it like it is.

'Oh, she was nice and smart but she broke my heart.' And Emily talks about her previous guys, and it's cool. They sound like cool dudes, only I'm cooler – obviously.

If you want my honest advice, take it slowly. Don't dive into the 'WAS YOUR EX SEXIER THAN ME WHEN SHE WAS AT THE BEACH IN A PEACH BIKINI?'

Ask the kind of questions you'd ask about someone's nan who recently died. 'Ah, was she a lovely person?'... 'Ah yeah, she sounded happy, was she happy?'

Y'know what I mean, horrible example but you get it, I hope...

'IF YOU WANT MY
HONEST ADVICE,
TAKE IT SLOWLY.'

EMILY'S VERSION

Well, ehm, okay, shit. AHA, sorry, I'm a little nervous because I don't want to lose my temper and say something silly, do I? Now, whenever I think about Cian's little girly-whirlies, I simply sit back and think, 'He went from them to me, he had a life upgrade and I am his prestigious gift' and then I feel really great about myself because I'm a fucking queen and will be forever worshipped as The Mothership.

Sorry, I got a little carried away there, eh... Cian's ex seems nice, I guess. She can't fucking do her eyeliner for shit but hey, let's not shame the un-gifted. I'll teach her someday, if she's lucky. One time I asked Cian about his ex and he got all flustered and started talking about butterflies or some shit, I don't know.

So whenever I ask about his beloved ex-girlfriend he turns into some tour guide in a butterfly museum telling me that butterflies have taste receptors on their feet. Like, I don't care, sweetie, I just want to know if your ex has bigger boobs than me.

Cian sometimes asks about my exes and I keep telling him that they were sexy as hell because I don't settle for any less. Cian seems to be the only one who can handle me, though. I mean, I am a human version of a deflating bouncy castle. I'm full of panic, terror and sheer mayhem. He cries most of the time while rocking back and forth in the corner throwing crucifixes at me and I never know why. He must be afraid from his previous relationships, who knows.

'I AM A HUMAN VERSION OF A DEFLATING BOUNCY CASTLE...'

CIAN v EMILY

Emily

Babeeee?

Cian

Yes darling?

Emily

You know the way you love me?

Cian

Yeah?

Emily

Well, did you love your ex more than you love me now?

Cian

...............what?

Emily

You heard me...

Cian

Did you know that there are over 15,000 different species of butterf...

Emily

I DON'T FUCKING CARE ABOUT HOW MANY FUCKING TYPES OF BUTTERFLIES ARE IN THE WORLD.

Cian

Alright, babe, calm down oh my God

Emily

Tell me about her.

Cian

Which one?

Emily

What...do...you...mean... which...one?

Cian

Yeah which one we got Sarah, we got Melanie, we have Katy, we have Chrisyshonbonaouiqua, we have Ste...

CIAN v EMILY

Emily

SHUT.......UP

Cian

what's wrong babe?

Emily

You're telling me that you're a pre-owned boyfriend?

Cian

Pre-owned? What do you mean?

Emily

I fucking found you when you were fresh and ripe. I never knew you were such a fucking man-whore.

Cian

Oh Emily for fuck sake just chill out please will you? You're over-reacting.

Emily

Please explain to me how I'm over-reacting.

Cian

I mean, an adult butterfly will eventually emerge from the chrysalis where it will wait a few hours for its wings to fill with blood and dry, before flying for the first time and...

Emily

STOP TRYING TO CHANGE THE FUCKING SUBJECT

Cian

Ugh, what do you want me to say babe?

Emily

Am I the best girlfriend you've ever had?

Cian

Of course you are, you're perfect.

Emily

mmmhmm, yeah thought so.

THE REAL STORY

If I am totally honest, whenever our previous partners come up in our conversation for whatever reason, neither of us get annoyed or pissed off with each other. I mean, no matter what we think of them now, they were still part of each of our lives at one point, and it's stupid to get all bitchy at the sound of their name. Just like this book, our lives have chapters. Don't get pissed off because someone else was there a few chapters before you. Be happy that you're able to be there in the present and accept the past!

At the same time, I wouldn't want to be in the same room as her previous guys, and I'm pretty sure Emily would love to join my exes in a room. She'd probably sit there and stare with a creepy smile and death-ray eyes. Just kidding, Emily has a gorgeous heart and a lovely personality (OMG, someone plz come help me, Emily is making me type this…).

WHEN YOUR GIRLFRIEND WANTS TO CELEBRATE A 'DAY YOU MET' ANNIVERSARY...

CIAN'S VERSION

When it comes to celebrating significant days in our relationship, Emily and I only celebrate our anniversary once a year. I asked her to be my girlfriend on Valentine's Day because I'm really fucking original. I hit two birds with one stone by asking her out on a day we'd be celebrating anyway. I'm like the guru on relationship budgeting: one bouquet of roses for two celebrations, win–win! I'm just kidding. I treat Emily like the fucking queen she is, bless her.

If your partner doesn't celebrate your yearly anniversary, I'd find that kind of shitty. Fair enough if you both don't want to do anything but if you really want to do something romantic or fun and your partner doesn't, that's lame. It takes two to tango and if your partner doesn't want to celebrate

being with you then give them a good dramatic argument (don't, actually).

Some couples celebrate their relationship monthly: 'OMG, babe, happy 45th month together.' I'm all for that at the beginning, like, the for first 12 months. But you can't go up to your grandkids when it's your 50th anniversary and be like 'Oh, kids, your granddad and I have been together for 600 months now, isn't that just fucking beautiful and exhaustingly accurate?'

Usually Emily gets me a little gift and I kind of provide the entire day. Last year we went to Paris for our first anniversary. Cute ,right? We ate sandwiches in the hotel room and refused to socialise in any public outing in France. It was perfect. Just how we like it, boring as fuck.

EMILY'S VERSION

So you've just finished reading my boyfriend Cian's amazing advice. Ladies, if you're going to listen to that shit then you deserve to be miserable, for fuck sake. I like to celebrate my relationship daily, if possible – that means I'm legally entitled to roses, teddy bears and dinner every fucking day.

I'm a princess, you see. AH HAAAAA yeaaah...

Y'all better be getting super-fucking-spoiled on your yearly anniversary. Cian brought me to shitty Paris for our first year. I originally wanted to go to the Maldives for six weeks with 200 sausage dogs and a Louis Vuitton handbag signed by Louis himself and all he does is bring me to shitty Paris? Don't suffer like I did. He even gave me some shit flowers that smelled like ass after two days. This year he'd better buy me a fucking pony that has a similar haircut to me so we can travel to beaches together and look flawless for the paparazzi.

Some people say I'm only in it for the gifts and presents. Well, they don't realise all the things I do for him, like when I'm using the toilet I flush it so he can use it later on if he wishes. See! I am considerate, my presence is enough of a present to him, baby.

CIAN v EMILY

EMILY, YOU CAN'T BE TELLING PEOPLE HOW
TO LIVE THEIR LIVES. THAT WAS SHIT ADVICE!

OH BOO-FUCKING-HOO, CIAN, I'M JUST VENTING TO MY
AMAZING FANS ON HOW SHIT YOU ARE AS A LIFE PARTNER.
YOU'RE DOING NOTHING THAT YOU SAID YOU'D DO IN THE CONTRACT.

WHAT CONTRACT?

THE CONTRACT, REMEMBER? THE ONE YOU SIGNED
AT THE BEGINNING OF OUR RELATIONSHIP?

I... I DIDN'T S—

OH, BUT YOU DID.... WHEN YOU WERE SLEEPING I SIGNED IT ON YOUR
BEHALF BECAUSE I DON'T MIND HELPING YOU OUT WITH YOUR BUSY LIFE.

EMILY, YOU CAN'T JUST SIGN A CONTRACT ON MY BEHALF.

YEAH, WELL... I DID, PUMPKIN, SO SUCK IT UP.

WHATEVER. ANYWAY YOU CAN'T BE GIVING
THAT KIND OF ADVICE TO PEOPLE READING THIS.

I WAS JUST GIVING THEM MY OPINION, CIAN. YOU TOLD ME TO BE HONEST.

YEAH, I DID, BUT I DIDN'T EXPECT YOU
TO BE THAT SELFISH, YOU'RE CRAZY.

DO NOT CALL ME CRAZY.

I'M N—

STOP TALKING.

...

GOOD BOY. NOW, DON'T YOU EVER RAISE YOUR VOICE AT ME EVER AGAIN.

BUT YOU WERE—

I SAID, STOP GODDAMN TALKING, DARLING.

OKAY...

I'M PUTTING WHATEVER I WANT INTO THIS BOOK, WATCH:
I'M GOING TO TYPE, 'FUCK OFF, CIAN' INTO THE BOTTOM OF THE
PAGE AND THERE'S NOTHING YOU'RE GOING TO DO ABOUT IT.

THE REAL STORY

I know that in the last little piece I just wrote, I mentioned that I went to Paris with Emily, well, that was a lie. I think I brought her to Paris as a little pre-anniversary gift, because I'm just such a perfect fucking boyfriend. On our actual anniversary, we used a Christmas present from my manager to stay at this fancy-ass resort place in Cork. I shit you not, Kanye West and Kim Kardashian stayed there as a part of their honeymoon. So basically since staying there I am just as cool as Kanye West. Also, if you're standing there shaking your head thinking Kanye West is shit, Kanye West is a fucking hero. I know all his songs word for word. Ultimate fucking fan here.

Anyway, let's not get side-tracked for the 300th time. We stayed in the big fancy place drinking fancy champagne and eating fancy food like cheese and shit. We had a great time: we relaxed, ate too much food and just enjoyed being away from the real world for a day. It didn't matter that we were in a big fancy-ass place. What mattered was we were there together, laughing. I'll probably take her away to Italy for the next one. Who doesn't want nothing but pizza and pasta all day? I'll be living the dream!

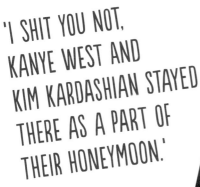

'I SHIT YOU NOT, KANYE WEST AND KIM KARDASHIAN STAYED THERE AS A PART OF THEIR HONEYMOON.'

WHEN YOU ADMIT TO YOUR GIRLFRIEND THAT YOU FANCY HER BEST MATE...

If you meet your girlfriend's friends and you tell her that you think one of them is gorgeous, you're a fucking plank. A big thick plank of shit, destined to be alone for the rest of your time on this planet. Too far? Nah, man, you cannot do that, dude. Although appreciating another person's visual appearance is totally cool, you cannot – and I fucking mean CANNOT – say they're attractive, good-looking, sexy, beautiful, etc. You want to know why, motherfucker? Because your partner is the only attractive, good-looking, sexy, and beautiful person you should be fucking looking at, goddamnit! Even if you think you need to say it, you don't. You don't sit at a restaurant and look at someone's grilled filet mignon with herb butter & Texas toast and tell them that their grilled filet mignon with herb butter & Texas toast is attractive, good-looking, sexy, and beautiful, when you have your own fucking grilled filet mignon with herb butter & Texas toast right in front of you!

I know that was a terrible example but, like I said before, I am not fucking qualified to do this shit. Some weird book person approached me and told me to write this book or I'm going to have bad luck for seven years and man I am not taking that chance, fuck that. Even though my example was rather shit, as usual. You still got the picture, worship your partner, not their friend.

EMILY'S VERSION

My bf is right with this one, I'm afraid to admit. IF he EVER came into MY home and complimented one of MY FRIENDS, he'd be single faster than I can run from the seat to the fridge, and baby that's 3.68 seconds, so don't fuck with me, yeah?

I can see why the question is here though because whenever one of the girls brings back a prisoner— I, eh, I mean, boy. Boyfriend, yeah. Anyway, whenever one of the girls brings a prisoner to be judged and tested by all of us, they always look at me and say, 'OH MY GOODNESS, QUEEN EMILY, YOUR EYES ARE JUST B-E-A-UTIFUL.'

People say it a lot because I'm perfect, flawless, etc. I think Cian never says anything about my girlies because I'm evidently the most beautiful person both in my group of friends and in the entire world, so I don't worry much there. If you're super ugly then yeah, fucking worry away, but if you're as sexy as I am, then why are you even reading this piece-of-shit book? Why aren't you out there making make-up tutorials and just SLAYING the fucking world?

To conclude my above statement, I find the best advice is: if you're ugly, worry. If you're not ugly, slay.

CIAN v EMILY

FRANTICALLY STORMING THROUGH HIS HOME
EMILY, WHERE THE FUCK ARE YOU?

I'M IN THE DINING ROOM. I JUST
FINISHED WRITING TO MY FANS, BABE. WHY?

YOU JUST TOLD EVERYONE THAT THEY
NEED TO WORRY IF THEY'RE UGLY?

YEAH. AND?

AND? THE PUBLISHERS ARE GOING TO
FUCKING KILL ME BECAUSE YOU'RE
WRITING UTTER SHIT INTO THIS!

UTTER SHIT? EXCUSE MOI?

YEAH, YOU CAN'T TELL PEOPLE THINGS LIKE THAT.
HOW MANY TIMES DO I HAVE TO REPEAT MYSELF!

CIAN, BABE, RELAX. IT'S NOT LIKE ANYONE IS
GOING TO READ THIS PIECE OF SHIT ANYWAY.

OH, OKAY, WHAT IS THAT SUPPOSED TO FUCKING MEAN?

IT MEANS, WITHOUT MY HELP THIS
BOOK WILL FLOP FASTER THAN I DO
AFTER A THREE-MINUTE RUN.

EMILY, THE ONLY REASON I OFFERED FOR YOU TO HELP
WAS SO YOU WOULD SHUT THE FUCK UP FOR TWO HOURS
A DAY WHILE YOU TYPE YOUR THOUGHTS.

AND THATS EXACTLY WHAT I'VE BEEN
FUCKING DOING, YOU WASTE OF LIFE.

YOU REALLY DON'T KNOW HOW FORTUNATE YOU ARE
TO HAVE ME, SO PLEASE STOP TREATING ME LIKE THIS.

AH HA! THAT'S CUTE, HOW AM I SO FORTUNATE?

BECAUSE I NEVER LOOK AT OTHER GIRLS AND WHAT I SAID
IN MY ADVICE SECTION WAS ALL TRUE — NOT MANY GUYS
WOULD DO THAT.

BABE, THE ONLY REASON YOU DON'T LOOK AT OTHER GIRLS
IS BECAUSE YOU KNOW THAT YOU'LL BE SHOT IN THE FOOT
WITH A HUNTING RIFLE FASTER THAN YOU CAN SAY, 'OMG,
THAT GIRL IS SUPER CUTE' SO DON'T STAND THERE LYING
TO ME, SUNSHINE.

OKAY.

GOOD BOY. NOW, ON TO THE NEXT PIECE.

THE REAL STORY

When I met Emily, my group of friends were like Versace topless models and I was the chubby nerdy guy in the background handing them water. Well, at least that's what it felt like, so you could imagine bringing my future girlfriend into a room full of guys that were sculpted by the gods. Luckily, Emily didn't have any interest in any of them, praise the fucking Lord, oh my yes! (Sorry, lads.)

Luckily, all of my friends respect me and when they see that I'm committing to a girl, they stay clear and respect my wishes to stay the fuck away from her! Believe it or not I've seen people steal other's girlfriends with ease, which fucking baffles me. So you can never be too safe – trust nobody!

When I first met Emily's friends I was fucking nervous. I knew that her girl group of friends were super protective. So walking into a room full of them felt like walking out to a courtroom being innocent and getting accused of murder. I did nothing wrong, but I was still shitting myself.

As I practically fell in love with Emily instantly, any girl that looked in my direction became invisible to me. I won the grand prize and nothing else compared. So Emily never really had to worry about me fancying any of her friends!

WHEN YOU HAVE TO DECIDE WHERE TO TAKE HER ON YOUR FIRST/SECOND/THIRD/FOURTH DATE....

Trying to figure out where to take your partner can be difficult, but just remember: if you have 'the one' coming along with you, any setting or activity will be magic. Luckily, when I met Emily, I'd already talked to her online for a month before we met face to face. So when it came to actually meeting her, we already knew each other pretty well. But if you're going on a date and you don't know each other well, then the best thing is dinner or a walk – you could even bring your fucking dog along too!

Moral of the story: take your date somewhere where you can talk to them, don't sit in silence watching a really shit fucking movie in the theatre for two hours then talking about the movie for four minutes after it's over, resulting in you making 0 fucking per cent of progress, goddamn it.

Having a car makes life a shit load easier for everyone and you don't have to spend a fortune on taxis. If your plan goes to shit, at least you can just drive elsewhere to save the date! Back in my day, we didn't have those fancy cars you kids drive around in all the time, we had to use our goddamn feet. So yeah, to conclude my fucking wonderful advice as to where you should bring your future partner, let it be a mutual decision. So at least if the restaurant you both picked was fucking dreadful, you could both laugh about it. But if it's just your idea and it fails, you look like a big loser who can't date for shit.

I'm only kidding... yeah.

EMILY'S VERSION

Ehm... okay, so yeah, here **coughs** is my advice on where to go for the first date with your future husband.

Step 1: Make sure wherever you go, you don't pay a single fucken cent, okay? You need to show the world that you're a queen! I don't think the Queen Bee Beyoncé has to pay for her dates! Be Beyoncé, be Sasha Fierce, my lovely little bitches... eh, sorry, I got a little carried away, ah ha. Oopsies.

Step 2: Make sure you look really cool and relaxed. That way he'll think you're slaying at the dating game and he will think you're some kind of goddess. Trust me, it works, ladies.

Step 3: If you're going to a restaurant, please make sure to prepare some questions for conversation, such as 'how much do you bench in the gym' and 'what's your credit card number?' I use these wonderful questions to get to know my date. I don't know their surname but at least I know their blood type, financial details and family medical history, lol.

If you think that this advice will help you, you can thank me all you want at my Twitter: @CianIsMyBitch. That is where I creep on Cian when he is not at home, troll little jealous bitches that hate on my swag, compliment celebrities in hope of them replying, and of course mute any bitches who try to steal my baby Cian's booty from me. His ass is mine, ladies, so back off.

CIAN V EMILY

Cian

Hahaha, babe you never did any of them things you told people you've done.

Emily

OH YEAH?!? Like what?

Cian

You didn't prepare any questions for me when we went for a meal for the first time. You just stared at me intensely while eating BBQ ribs.

Emily

I was fucking flirting with you, Cian, for fuck sake!

Cian

Who the fuck flirts with someone by intensely staring at them while eating fucking BBQ ribs!?

Emily

I've told you many times that I am unique and now you have a perfect example as to why I'm such a rare lil human.

Cian

You're not that rare... Emily, what are you doing?

Emily

Look, babe, I can clean my ears using some tissue on my toes.

Cian

Emily, get up please, for fuck sake.

Emily

AH HA, two more reasons as to why I'm unique as fuck!

Cian

Ugh, we're going off topic. I'm saying you're not that honest with your advice!

Emily

Okay, ehm... why would you say I'm not honest, my delicious little hubby?

Cian

You're not honest because you haven't fucking done anything! You didn't let me pay for your meal at all, you just pretended you had food poisoning and made the manager not charge us for our food!

Emily

And till this day you still haven't fucking said thank you!

THE REAL STORY

I'm going to be super fucking honest with you people here, okay? I legit do not remember what Emily and I did for our first date. Simply because we did nothing in the first stages of our relationship. I mean, would you consider standing around with a lot of grown men talking about EK9 Civics? No, you don't.

(By the way, for anyone that doesn't know what an EK9 Civic is, it's a Honda car that makes a shit-ton of fucking noise. It sounds like a hairdryer that's moments away from exploding.)

Our first 'date' that I can remember is our second time we ever met. We lay in my bed (with clothes on, you filthy freak) and we watched *American Horror Story*, Season 2 to be exact. She cuddled into me and my butterflies turned into viscous bullet ants. I fell in love that night, because I'm a ball of cringe and emotion. Fuck my life.

WHEN YOUR GIRLFRIEND ASKS YOU WHAT YOU ORIGINALLY LIKED ABOUT HER... CIAN'S VERSION

As some of you know, I said I met Emily at a wine and cheese convention in the South of France. Well, when I said that I assumed that people would realise that it was a joke. Well, people took it up and thought it was 'destined' that we met and all that other spiritual shit your aunt rants on about when she's pissed on two bottles of wine on Christmas Day. Well, anyway, I fear Emily and I didn't actually meet at a wine and cheese convention in the South of France, in fact we met on....**Please prepare yourself. Readers discretion is advised**

I, eh, I met Emily... the love of my life... on… Tinder.

Yeah, I fucking said it, on Tinder, the dating app. Yeah, that one, with the orange flame thingy as its logo. Yeah that one.

When I first saw pictures of Emily I was hook, line and sinker'd within 0.8 seconds. So of course I poured my compliments all over the table and shoved them in her arms to take in.

Always compliment your companion, whether now or in 80 years' time when you both look like a pair of testicles, call her beautiful. They'll forever cherish that.

Do what I didn't, make sure you don't sound too nice. You'll end up looking like a fucking creep, like I did. Oops, sorry Emily.

EMILY'S VERSION

When I met Cian on Tinder I thought he looked super cute so I instantly ignored him until he called me sxc or something, and he did after 0.8 seconds, which was just superperfect. I live by the saying 'Being stubborn makes you more sexy so don't say nothing until you're complimented'. I think it was Marilyn Monroe who said that or Meryl Streep, no Marilyn Manson...eh, I don't know, someone fucking famous said it so it must be true, right?

Calling Cian beautiful makes me want to vomit all of my pasta carbonara on the white tiles in my kitchen so personally I do not compliment him, unless he looks sad or something. So sometimes I'll call him Champ and rub his ear, in a similar way to Max,

my Jack Russell. I treat Max and Cian very similarly, only Cian's collar is orange and Max's is blue.

Everything that Cian is saying is kind of true. He did compliment me a lot which made me turn red in the face like a fresh water malone. What? It's pronounced 'malone', Oh... melon? What the fuck is a watermelon? Oh, is that how you say it? Ah ha, okay, whatever. Yeah, he was super cute and called me scrumptious and said my eyes looked like two diamonds or some cringe shit like that. Super cute, but also super lame. Girls I do think you should say some cute shit to your partner sometimes, call him a big hairy hunk or something. He'll curl up in a little ball similar to a crab fighting the water currents.

SXC

> I live by the saying 'Being stubborn makes you more sexy so don't say nothing until you're complimented'.

CIAN v EMILY

YOU NEVER COMPLIMENT ME.

ER, YES I DO, ACTUALLY!

BABE, I WON'T LIE. I DON'T THINK I CAN
EVER RECALL A SINGLE MOMENT WHEN YOU CALLED
ME BEAUTIFUL OR HANDSOME OR WHATEVER. YOU
KNOW GUYS LIKE TO FEEL PRETTY TOO, DON'T YOU?

AH HA HA HA HA!

...

HA HAAAAAAAAOOOHHHHHH... OH MY, OH YOU'RE BEING
SERIOUS, OH SHIT, OKAY PUMPKIN, EHM, I EH... I THINK
YOU ARE LIKE, SUPER CUTE AND STUFF.

OH... YOU DO? **GIGGLES WHILE
PULLING CHIN IN TO CHEST**

EH YEAHHHH, SURE? OF COURSE,
I DO DARLING, YOU DA CUTEST.

OH, HOLY HELL. BABE YOU BETTER STOP,
YOU'RE MAKING ME BLUSH. MY FACE WILL
LOOK LIKE A WATER MALONE.

ACTUALLY, BABE, IT'S PRONOUNCED 'WATERMELON'.
I MADE THE MISTAKE MYSELF WHEN A RUDE LITTLE
BITCH INTERVENED AND TOLD ME THE CORRECT
WAY TO SAY IT WAS MELON.

OH, WOW, OKAY. I DIDN'T KNOW
THAT. GUESS WHAT?

WHAT?

NO, YOU HAVE TO GUESS!

I, EH, I DON'T KNOW....

C'MON...

I DON'T FUCKING KNOW,

OH, OKAY BABE, SORRY, I WAS GOING
TO SAY THAT YOU ARE BEAUTIFUL.

AW, BABY, THANK YOU, THAT'S SO NICE.

SO, EH, DO YOU THINK I'M BEAUTIFUL?

AH HAAA, STOP NOW, BABE... DON'T ASK ME THAT...
FACE CLENCHES UP WHILE EMILY GRABS HER STOMACH

TELL ME I'M BEAUTIFUL!

NO NO! DON'T DO THIS!

TELL ME!

NOOOOOOO!

AHHHHHHHHHHHH!

AHHHHH, YOU'RE BEAUTIFULLLLLL!

**EMILY PROCEEDS TO VOMIT HER PASTA CARBONARA
ALL OVER THE WHITE TILES IN THE KITCHEN**

THE REAL STORY

It's got to the stage where I compliment Emily every couple of hours. She could be in the toilet taking a huge shit and I'd just randomly intervene and call her beautiful. She would just sit there and awkwardly thank me, then proceed to ask me to leave. Back when I first met Emily I was afraid to compliment her. Sure, texting her on my phone was easy. You can call someone beautiful all day when you're texting them, but in person it's fucking terrifying.

'EMILY, YOU ARE FUCKING GORGEOUS, OKAY?'

'Ehmm, okayyyy?'

See? Fucking horribly awkward, kill me now. After some time, I developed a habit of just complimenting her at the oddest moments. Sitting in the church at a funeral: 'You look lovely today.' What the fuck, Cian? Why would you say it at such an inconsiderate time?! I don't fucking know, dude, I'm sorry, don't give me the evil eyes because I was complimenting Emily so I could be at ease! I couldn't hold it in any more.

HELLO SCRUMPTIOUS

WHEN YOU FIRST STARTED FLIRTING WITH HER AND THEN IT BECAME REALLY WEIRD...

Flirting is a minefield of emotions. Saying the wrong thing like, 'I think your boobies are delicious-looking', is probably going to score you little to no points. Focus on the respectful things you big fucking dickhead, like her eyes and lips, etc.

Here is one of my classics: 'Hey girl, your green eyes remind me of my childhood because they're the same shade of wallpaper as my bedroom when I was four years old.'

Usually I'll have charmed the woman so much that we'd just pop in a blu-ray and talk about emotions. Emily is a lucky girl isn't she?

From personal experience, if I felt awkward in the first place, the last thing I'd do is fuck it up even more with some cheesy-ass compliment about her forehead or some shit. Yeah, Cian, let's just sit down in a lovely restaurant and talk to her about how perfectly symmetrical her face is.

Usually I wait a little to flirt even though it is more of an ice-breaker than global-warming. Emily was impossible not to flirt with. It's like I caught a really fucking rare Pokemon and had to throw my balls at her as fast and as hard as possible without losing her. I'm talking about my Pokeballs, you sick freaks, if you want that kinky kind of shit you need to head back to the airport shop where you bought this book, return it and buy some really weird kinky book. But for this book, I'm talking about fucking Pokemon, okay? So as I was saying, I was lobbing all of my balls straight at Emily...

EMILY'S VERSION

Flirting, ah. Something that not many can master. It is a hidden language that was devised by the Greek god Zanzibar (I have no idea if that's a Greek god, please do excuse my lack of knowledge). But anyway, it's real fucken rare and super hard to do. Luckily you purchased this book and I myself happen to be a fucken guru when it comes to this shit, okay, people?

So sit back a little and get ready for the best advice you have ever been given.

I want you to imagine this scene. You're at a bar. You're on your fifth cookie. You're feeling a little woozy from the sugar rush. All of a sudden, a guy approaches. He's

not just any guy, but it's fucken Ryan Gosling **cues multiple girls making weird moaning noises to indicate that Ryan is in fact a very charming and attractive human**

He walks right up to you and says, 'Hey baby, wanna go for a ride?'

DO NOT REPLY BY SAYING, 'Sure, Ken.' You simply reply by saying, 'Fuck off, you dirty pervert, I'm just trying to enjoy my cookie.'

If he leaves, then he was not the one. But if he returns with another cookie, he's a keeper.

Ryan never returned, and now I'm stuck with Cian.

'IF HE LEAVES, THEN HE WAS NOT THE ONE. BUT IF HE RETURNS WITH ANOTHER COOKIE, HE'S A KEEPER.'

CIAN v EMILY

Cian

You ungrateful little bitch.

Emily

Oh Jesus, someone sounds a little fucking sassy this morning.

Cian

RYAN? Who the fuck is Ryan?

Emily

Whoa, it seems the tables have turned and there's a giant twist in this book.

Cian

Stop being so fucking sarcastic with me for once. Tell me – are you in love with Ryan?

Emily

He didn't return with a cookie, Cian. You buy me shit all the time, so obviously I be loving you way more.

Cian

You're a gold-digger.

Emily

Eh, no I'm not, I have my own money.

Emily turns purse upside-down revealing the contents of her purse

Cian

See?

Emily

Eh, excuse you, I have 26 cents, a button and a half-eaten Easter Egg. So think before you speak, bitch.

THE REAL STORY

Emily and I began flirting instantly, it was one of the main elements of our Tinder conversation. I mean, you don't talk about the global economic downfall and the effects it has on today's society when you're chatting someone up now, do you? Now, we weren't like, 'hey sexy, send me a picture of your willy xxx' kind of flirting. We were more or less flirting unintentionally, but intentionally, you get me? She'd talk about her day and what she did and it somehow sounded sexy. Weird, right? We always had the stereotypical, 'Aww, I'd love a cuddle' type of shit, but it worked. It made her interesting and I felt obliged to keep the conversation going. I don't think she was intentionally flirting at times, but she was good at it.

THE FIRST DATES

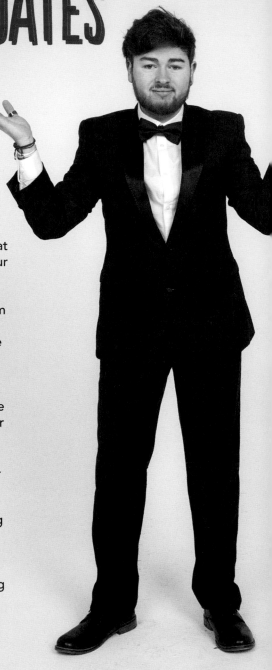

Before we begin talking about this can I just ask what even is a date? Like, is it a romantic meal with some fine wine and maybe a delicate smooch after? Or is it just Emily and I smashing our faces into burgers and hysterically laughing at one another with ketchup all around our mouths? Either way, I have no fucking idea what a date is, so what I'll do is consider our first time alone a 'date'.

It came about quite uneventfully, if I'm honest. I'm not going to sit here and type words that didn't happen for the sheer purpose of entertainment, am I? No, of course not. Our first date was fighting a local gang down in the alleyway who didn't like my shoes. We fought 12 bodybuilders using only our flip-flops as weapons. I was wearing shoes at the time but always keep a spare pair of flip-flops in my lavender-scented man purse.

If you can't tell by now, I'm not being serious here. There was only nine of them...

Our first 'date' was the two of us lying in bed watching *American Horror Story*. I know that doesn't sound like a date, but fuck you and your entire family if you want to judge me on what I consider a date. Oh, forgive me, for I may have lost my composure there. There's a hint of my alter ego coming out of me... FUCK YOU, BITCH. Emily leave me be, I'm trying to write this book. YEAH YEAH, WHATEVER, JUST WAKE ME WHEN YOU'RE DONE.

Okay! Christ, sorry about this, guys, she's really inconsiderate at times. So, where were we? Oh yeah the 'date'.

So by now you're aware that Emily and I are a Tinder couple. Yes, we met on a dating app, get the fuck over it. So we spent a few weeks talking before we actually met. After we first met up in person I was worried that she didn't like me or whatever because I ain't the prettiest lily in the bouquet and she was. It was like a rose being attracted to a dirty little daisy with some dog shit on it.

After Emily went home that first time she didn't text me for about eight hours, the reason being that was she was asleep. Like, how selfish of her to nap after her long and exhausting day of having to deal with me for a few hours. I never knew how she did it.

The next day I was awoken by a 'Hello there' text from Emily.

PRAISE THE FUCKING LORDS, SHE ACTUALLY WANTS TO CONTINUE TO TALK TO ME! FUCK YEAH, CIAN!

Emily suggested that she would like to come down to Cork to see me again, so I guess you could say that she asked me out on a date! Fuck. Yes. 'Of course I want you to come down. What time is the bus?'

When Emily arrived we decided what we wanted to do for our first time alone together. I know that sounds creepy so if there's any creepy dudes out there waiting to see if I touched her boob, you're wasting your time. She suggested that we relax and watch a movie, and that's my favourite type of date. No need to dress up, it's not expensive and I can fart freely into the atmosphere without being asked to leave by a member of staff. So yeah, we watched *American Horror Story*. Emily had already seen it all but she insisted that I'd love it. It was actually quite boring for me but I pretended that I loved it so it was another thing I could talk about with her. Look at me being thoughtful and shit. Bless my cotton socks.

Now I will admit, I have seen every episode of *American Horror Story* and I did eventually get hooked and I became morbidly obsessed with it.

If you're unfamiliar with *American Horror Story*, it's kind of like the directors took a shit-ton of acid and cocaine, closed their eyes and smashed their heads onto a keyboard until they created a TV show, and for some reason it's perfect. If you like really fucked-up shit with weird people coming out of mattresses trying to eat your ass cheeks for dinner then this is the fucking show for you, my friends.

My first impression of Emily when I met her was that she was perfect: she wasn't some fake person who fake laughed at every joke to seem polite, she was honest and had the exact same personality as me. She was super funny and had the mouth of a sailor. Listening to the two of us arguing might have more profanity in it than every Eminem song combined. The most important thing I noticed is that she made me feel comfortable,

I didn't have to put on this fake front bullshit to act all cool and whatever, she just accepted me for the weird little freak that I am, and I love her for that. Thanks for letting me be weird, darling.

'SHE'S SUPER HONEST, FUNNY AND HAS THE MOUTH OF A SAILOR.'

Initially I was petrified as this was my first time being alone with Emily. At least when I first met her I had my friends with me to soften the potential awkwardness, which didn't happen thankfully. We ate double cheeseburgers in a car park and talked about gherkins. I did the sneaky yawn to try get my arm around Emily but by the time I was mid yawn she already had her head on my chest. I think that was the first moment I started feeling emotions towards her and shit. Super-cute, right?

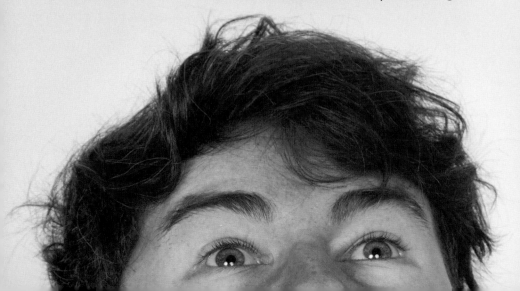

WHEN YOU TALK ABOUT BECOMING GIRLFRIEND AND BOYFRIEND...

I'm one of them guys who could spend months trying to pluck up the courage to ask a girl to be my girlfriend (not that I've done it often). But having to ask a girl like Emily to be my girlfriend was something that I was never taught how to do in school. How does a chubby little monster ask a sexy lil Emily to be my girlfriend? I didn't fucking know. She constantly dropped me hints like, 'Oh, you should totally fucking ask me to be your fucking girlfriend, you sack of shit. Where the fuck is the question?' and 'What the fuck is your problem, you ugly fucking ball-bag?'

See? They were clearly minor hints, but as I mentioned previously, I decided to ask her to be my girlfriend on Valentine's Day – kind of a twofer anniversary/VD celebration every year. As soon as I asked her there were tears everywhere supplied by the amazing Emily, even the odd snot bubble. You would think she'd be half expecting it on Valentine's Day, but noooooo, of course she didn't. I kinda caught her off guard, I think. Well, at least with her reaction it gave me the impression that she was totally caught off guard, like a zebra calmly sipping some water from the pond until a giant fucking alligator comes out of nowhere and snatches the zebra right into a headlock. That kind of 'off guard'.

WHEN YOU GO OUT ON YOUR SECOND OR THIRD DATE...

As you've already discovered, I cannot tell what is and what isn't considered a 'date'. So to narrow all of this down into a neat little paragraph to save you, the lovely reader, from going into a pit of repetition and complete misery, instead of talking about Emily and I going on multiple 'dates' let's just call it 'being in the fucking presence of each other'.

We were used to being in the fucking presence with each other a lot since our *American Horror Story* marathon. Emily would get her naïve father to drop her to college only to then hop on a bus and travel two hours to me every day. Yep, what a keeper.

We went from watching *American Horror Story* to watching *Home Alone* 300 times by mid-February. We both still couldn't believe Christmas was over so we had to rely on young Kevin and the rest of the McCallister family to keep that little Christmas spirit glowing. After we noticed that pizza existed, we began having pizza parties. The only rule was that no one else was invited because fuck sharing pizza, man, get your own fucking slice.

Emily gets pepperoni and red onion, while I get ham and pineapple. What the fuck are you going to do? Judge me? HA! Nah man, go live your miserable life elsewhere and leave me and my Hawaiian to get on with our lives. **spits on floor with disrespect to anyone who doesn't accept pineapple as a topping**

Now, as you may notice, I have a bit of a following on Facebook. When I met Emily I had 196,000 followers, to be exact. I only remember that number because I was stuck on 196,000 for around six months. When we announced 'publicly' on Facebook, I forgot to ask Emily if she was okay to be shown to 196,000 people as my girlfriend. Of course she didn't mind but as soon as I posted that we were now a 'thing' she began getting hundreds of friend requests and shit. Emily was like a full-blown celebrity. **please notice the sarcasm in that sentence, you cynical asshole**

We kind of had no idea that us being a couple would later turn into some incredibly random and fucked-up career for the both of us.

Aww so cute, pardon me while I vomit under my desk.

In a relationship

In a Relationship

Cian Twomey and Emily Rochford are in a relationship

Like · Comment

THE CIAN AND EMILY Q&A — PART ONE

You know the drill, dipshits. I make up some questions that hopefully will help some of you out and I can then pretend to be a qualified relationship counsellor.

HOW DO I KNOW IF I'M A GOOD KISSER?

CIAN

Well, you won't find out by sitting in the corner of the room rocking back and forward practising how to bite someone's lip using a teddy bear as a stand-in partner. You're just going to have to go out into the big bad world to find someone who is willing to kiss you and let you bite their lip and stuff. I straight up just asked Emily if I was a good kisser and she told me that I was. Of course she had to tell me that. Imagine asking:

'So, ehhhh... do you think I'm a good kisser?'

'Meh, you're okay, yeah.'

'Oh... oh well, okay, ehm... ha ha. **scratches head** Thanks, I guess.'

'Oh no, it wasn't a complim—'

'But I was practising with my teddy bear.' **pulls out 'Teddy' the teddy bear**

I'm quite confident with my kissing. I mean, anytime I kiss Emily she runs as far away as possible from me, probably because she is just so overwhelmed with how amazing my luscious lips are. Either that or she just finds me utterly repulsive and is only going out with me because I have a blue verified tick on all my social media accounts. I mean, me and my verified accounts are pretty badass so I don't blame her for being with me because she has a swag-ass boyfriend who gets all the ladies.

But yeah, to sum up all the bullshit I just wrote, if you want to know if you're a good kisser; just fucking ask the person you kissed.

Ask and you shall receive.

'EITHER THAT OR SHE JUST FINDS ME UTTERLY REPULSIVE AND IS ONLY GOING OUT WITH ME BECAUSE I HAVE A BLUE VERIFIED TICK ON ALL MY SOCIAL MEDIA ACCOUNTS.'

EMILY

If you want to know if you're a good kisser, just make a pizza and if you can eat all of the pizza without getting any sauce around your mouth, you should be fine.

CIAN v EMILY

Cian

Emily, that was the poorest example to give to someone who is asking for advice on kissing.

Emily

Oh great, here he fucking is again. Interrupting me as I type sheer art into this computer screen.

Cian

I'm not. This is my book and I don't want you to start fucking it all up.

Emily

Y'know what, babe? Why don't you just fuck off into the toilet and take the biggest shit of your life.

Cian

I don't need to use the bathroom.

Emily

Well, you're standing here with enough shit coming out of your mouth I just assumed you needed to take a giant poo. Just fuck off and leave me alone. Okay, sexy?

Cian

But...

Emily

Thanksssss, buh byeeee

WHAT IF I'M A MESSY EATER?

CIAN

I personally like it when Emily doesn't give a shit who is looking at her while she eats. I've been on a date where the girl literally ate her chips/fries with a knife and fork. After each bite she then wiped her mouth ever so gently with a napkin. Emily, on the other hand, isn't quite like that. You see, Emily is one of them girls who can finish a half-pound burger with garlic and cheese fries before I even open my salt sachet. The girl just doesn't give a shit and I fucking adore that.

So I guess it just all goes down to the person you're with. If they can't accept you for how you eat, why haven't you left to find someone who's actually decent yet?

EMILY

Ya' see, whenever myself and Cian have a light snack like a family bucket from KFC or something, I tend to eat it quite elegantly. When I say elegantly, I mean I shovel the food so fast down my throat that I didn't even have time to fucking taste it.

So, ladies and gentlemen, if you're a messy eater and you're worried that your date will be repulsed by your messy ways, I feel you deserve better and you need to find someone who understands your messy needs. After all, you are the most polite version of yourself ever on your first date. So it only goes downhill and messier from here, buddy. I could go from eating a nice tapas salad and getting mayonnaise on my cheek to dipping chicken nuggets into my bellybutton filled with ketchup.

CIAN: EMILY, I'M ACTUALLY QUITE SURPRISED.

EMILY: WHY, BABE?

CIAN: BECAUSE, WELL, WE ACTUALLY GAVE OUT THE SAME ADVICE. WELL, YOU WERE MORE DESCRIPTIVE AND KIND OF DISGUSTING, BUT OUR POINTS WERE THE SAME.

EMILY: AH WELL, YOU KNOW WHAT THEY SAY...

CIAN: ...

EMILY: ...

CIAN: ... WHAT DO THEY SAY, BABE?

EMILY: OH, I DON'T KNOW I JUST THOUGHT IT WAS A COOL THING TO SAY.

SHOULD I INITIATE FOOTSIE UNDER THE TABLE ON A FIRST DATE?

CIAN

Y'know, correct me if I'm wrong, but I find that playing footsie is a thing of the past. I mean, yeah, I often scrape my toes off of Emily's ankle when we're going to sleep, but I certainly don't remove my shoe and caress her feet with my cotton socks while eating a chicken tikka mid-date. That's just fucking creepy, dude. But yeah, if that's your thing, just make sure the person you're planning to play footsie with is comfortable with it. I mean if a girl just started stroking my shin with her big toe I'd kindly ask her to get the fuck away from me. So yeah, just be like, 'Ehmmm, can I rub your ankle with my foot?'

EMILY

ON A FIRST FUCKING DATE? ARE YOU SERIOUS, MATE? Cian was lucky enough to have permission to bless me anytime I sneezed on our first date, let alone get his huge fucking lobster claws anywhere near my fresh tan. Stay well clear of this shit, ladies. Half the time when Cian tries to play footsie with me, I feel like throwing up in my mouth as it feels like a praying mantis trying to get up a steep tree. Fuck that, I'd rather have a spider lay its eggs in my eye sockets, thanks very much.

'CIAN WAS LUCKY ENOUGH TO HAVE PERMISSION TO BLESS ME ANYTIME I SNEEZED ON OUR FIRST DATE, LET ALONE GET HIS HUGE FUCKING LOBSTER CLAWS ANYWHERE NEAR MY FRESH TAN.'

CIAN: YOU SAID YOU LIKED IT WHEN I PLAY FOOTSIE WITH YOU?

EMILY: YEAH, AND I ALSO SAID I LIKED YOUR MOTHER'S COOKING, SO WOOPDIEFUCKINGDO, WE HAVE OURSELVES A JERRY SPRINGER MOMENT HERE, NOW, DON'T WE?

CIAN: YOU SAID YOU ALWAYS LOVED HER COOKING. HOW COULD YOU? MY MOTHER IS A SAINT..

EMILY: YEAH? WHICH SAINT IS SHE, CIAN? IS SHE THE FUCKING SAINT OF MISERABLE BAKING OR IS SHE THE SAINT OF I OVERCOOK EVERYTHING?

CIAN: YOU TAKE THAT BACK, YOU... SOUR LITTLE BITCH.

EMILY: GO FUCK YOURSELF CIAN, AND YOUR MOTHER'S LIFE.

WHAT CAN I DO ABOUT MY SWEATY HANDS?

CIAN

You know what? I haven't quite thought this through. Who the fuck would worry about their sweaty hands? It's natural, brah. It ain't like you worry if you need to take a shit or piddle mid-date. Or is that something that people worry about? Jesus Christ, I've just turned from the teacher to the student. Even I don't know if needing to take a poopie or a wee-wee mid-date is considered something to worry about. But what do you do? Do you sit there and wait while your internal organs erupt due to holding in your packages for too long? It's funny, actually, because as I'm writing this I just reminded myself that whenever Emily is sitting down with me and she needs to use the bathroom, without fail she will always let me know by saying, 'Gotta take a shit'.

She will say this whether it be on our own, with my family over for dinner, during my live-streams and constantly interrupting me when I'm trying to make a video.

Thanks for letting me know about that, Emily. But anyway, I know that I have gone off topic there. It may have been by accident or it may be because I have no fucking idea how to answer this question. Let's see if Emily knows.

EMILY

Thank you, Cian, that was a wonderful piece to tell us all here reading this amateur book written by a complete asshole who doesn't deserve this opportunity to publish a book. Don't you dare ever consider yourself an author. Anyway, my sexy ladies, Cian clearly doesn't understand that having sweaty palms is a big issue, especially when your knees are weak and your arms are heavy. Let's not forget Mom's spaghetti... (to quote my favourite poet).

Sweaty palms means everything is going to be slippery, this includes cutlery, and I hate it when my sweaty-ass hands make me drop my spoon of meatball sauce all over my bridal dress that I bring on all dates to show Cian what he's looking forward to. I can't afford to get sauce all over it. It costs more than two of my handbags from my collection.

My advice: wear gloves at all times. If he or she asks you about them, tell them to eat shit and die and not to ask such sensitive questions about your glove issue. Problem solved.

PART 2
MAKING THE
COMMITMENT

OUR FIRST FEW MONTHS TOGETHER...

CIAN'S VERSION

Usually in a relationship, you start off from scratch by not knowing each other in the fucking slightest. Once the days go by and the dates turn into them funky sleepover things, you begin to learn about the other person. Whether it be about their ex-partners or your joyful discovery of their third nipple, it doesn't matter, you still gather information about each other and develop a solid relationship together.

The start of a relationship is usually either the best part or the worst part. There are a few pros and cons to the first few months. You're either expressing your infinite love towards one another every second of the day like Ryan Gosling and Rachel McAdams in *The Notebook* or you can be like Angelina Jolie and Brad Pitt in *Mr and Mrs Smith*, where you scream and verbally assault the living fuck out of each other while smashing any vintage china plates and Waterford crystal bowls you could lay your hands on, then aggressively make love on the kitchen floor like two dogs in heat. Ain't that a fucking pretty sight? I think not.

'WHETHER IT BE ABOUT THEIR EX-PARTNERS OR YOUR JOYFUL DISCOVERY OF THEIR THIRD NIPPLE, IT DOESN'T MATTER...'

The first few months are always like a bit of a test drive. You make sure everything works and you're comfortable with it. Sadly, on the odd and rare occasion, people could end up showing a 'fake' side in the beginning of the relationship. This could simply be due to nerves and they could be trying to 'wow' you. Who fucking knows. Anyway, I've had a few friends who've run into situations where they fell in mad love with their partners who after a few months showed their true colours and turned out to be just plain nasty people. Kind of a shame, ain't it?

A lot of people have been hurt in the past. Maybe an ex cheated on them, which crushed their trust for any poor soul who tries to chance a relationship with them. Anyway, at the start it could be rocky. It's natural for humans to be paranoid, right? It could be as simple as wondering who they're laughing at when they texted them, to a simple 'Why did you just smile at that dude in the frozen meat section? Is he an ex- boyfriend you didn't tell me about!? Are you cheating on me?'

Maybe a little over the top, right? So yes, AS I WAS SAYING. There are a lot of amazing things that can happen within the first few months of your fresh and new relationship. For example, you could end up adapting to the other person's hobbies and interests. I mean, I know everything about fucking make-up and Emily is able to edit a full fucking video on Final Cut Pro. Neither of us would know that shit until we showed interest in each other's interests. Your partner might even have a few suggestions that might benefit you, such as, 'Darling, maybe you should wear black skinny jeans instead of blue skinny jeans.' Honestly, the best decision ever. I mean, black skinny jeans go with practically fucking anything.

We also worry that any previous lovers are lurking in the background like a creepy ass stalker like Tyler from 13 Reasons Why. If you haven't seen that show I highly fucking recommend it but don't watch it until you've finished this book because I don't want you having any fucking distractions, okay?

Other than that, the first few months are months to enjoy and learn to love a once stranger who is now your absolutely everything. It's pretty amazing ain't it?

EMILY'S VERSION

I've broken so many hearts in the past. It's usually because they piss me off or something, it's never my fault I promise. This one time a guy bought me a Pandora bracelet and didn't buy me any fucken charms to go with them. He was lucky that he kept the receipt for the bracelet and I was lucky that I kept the receipt for him. I brought him back to the bar where I found him three weeks beforehand.

My advice for the first few months is simple. If you're a girl, you should teach them while you're young and make them buy you as many gifts as possible. That way, if you suddenly don't like them any more, at least you have a hamper for cheese and wine and a new dress. Ha ha, they fall for it every time.

When I met Cian he swept me off my feet. Ahhh, I remember the day I first laid my eyes on his bank account. I was working in the driving test centre and he came in to get his licence renewed. I was required to ask for a bank statement for proof of address and then I saw it. It was so large – his bank account, I mean. Not his willy, that's fucken gross, you pervert.

As I was saying, I asked him for his digits. He popped them on a napkin and I called him that night and demanded he brought me to a fancy restaurant with some French guy cooking my food. Y'know, the French make good baguettes and French fries after all.

He took me out and he didn't even offer me a 12th glass of wine I was so fucken livid but I decided to give him a chance because he has a lot of moneyyyyyyyy. Personality. Yeah, personality. A lot of personality. Yeah. Ah ha. Fuck. What'll I say now? I've totally fucked this up. I'm sorry, Cian sweetie, please don't be mad at me.

Your first few months should be sexy and funky. Touch his bum in the mornings. Make him tickle your ankle with his crusty toe, be romantic like that. Leave your snotty tissues around and let him stand in it to get his day off to a horrible start. Argue with him constantly; call him a pussy for no reason. Eat his chocolate stash. Put salt in his coffee or something. If he's still there in the end of all of that, you've got yourself a lil bitch. And that's when you know you have a fucken keeper.

'TOUCH HIS BUM IN THE MORNINGS. MAKE HIM TICKLE YOUR ANKLE WITH HIS CRUSTY TOE, BE ROMANTIC LIKE THAT.'

CIAN v EMILY

EMILY, THAT WHOLE STORY ABOUT ME
AND YOU MEETING FOR THE FIRST TIME
IS COMPLETE BULLSHIT!

EH, HOW THE FUCK IS IT, CIAN? DO I SEEM LIKE
SOME KIND OF COMPULSIVE FUCKEN LIAR TO YOU?

WELL, NO BABE, BUT I DO FEEL LIKE IT'S A BAD IDEA TO LIE TO THE
PEOPLE WHO BOUGHT THIS BOOK AND ARE READING IT RIGHT NOW.

AH, FUCK THEM PEOPLE, IT'S THEIR OWN FAULT FOR BUYING A
FUCKING BOOK. YOU KNOW WHAT YOU COULD HAVE GOT INSTEAD
OF BUYING THIS BOOK? FORTY FUCKEN MCNUGGETS WITH SIX
FUCKEN DIPS. BUT INSTEAD THEY'RE READING THIS SHITTY-ASS
BOOK WRITTEN BY SOME WEIRD GUY WHO HAS SOME FUCKED-
UP ALTER EGO AND PEOPLE FIND IT ENTERTAINING FOR SOME
REASON. FUCK THEM, CIAN, AND FUCK YOU.

...

WHAT?

EMILY. WHY ARE YOU SO FUCKING HORRIBLE TO ME?

BECAUSE, CIAN, IT'S YOUR ANNUAL PATIENCE TEST, AH HA.

PATIENCE TEST? EMILY, YOU KNOW THAT YOU'RE SO CLOSE TO
BEING ABUSIVE IN THIS RELATIONSHIP. WHY DO YOU NEED TO FEEL
LIKE IT'S YOUR MISSION TO BE A TOTAL FUCKING BITCH?

SMILING OHHHHHH, YOU'RE IN FOR A REAL TREAT
ONCE I FINISH EATING THIS CROISSANT, BIG BOY.

TROUBLE?

AH HAAAA, YEAHHHH. YOU'VE GONE AND
FUCKED UP THIS TIME, BIG BOY.

YOU WERE NEVER LIKE THIS IN THE FIRST FEW MONTHS OF US BEING TOGETHER. YOU KNOW NOTHING ABOUT GIVING GOOD ADVICE.

I BET EVERYONE HERE ONLY BOUGHT THIS BOOK BECAUSE I'M THE FUCKING STAR. YOU SAY THIS AND THAT BUT IN REALITY YOU'RE ONLY HERE TO HOLD A CONVERSATION.

FUCK. YOU. EMILY.

GO. FUCK. YOURSELF. CIAN.

THE REAL STORY

Y'know, the first few months of being with Emily were pretty fucking cool. I mean, the first month of knowing her was just myself and her talking on Facebook and WhatsApp. The second month was when I met her. The things that developed in the first few months were:

TRUST

Although we knew we would never be unfaithful to each other, we still had trust issues and that's totally fucking normal. It's perfectly natural for someone to get protective and jealous if your partner's attention is momentarily drawn to another person. I never give Emily a reason not to trust me and Emily never gives me a reason either. We know we'd be lost without each other and nothing would be worth risking that. Fuck that.

UNDERSTANDING

Every couple has something they find irritating, annoying or just plain fucking painful to sit through. In the first months of being together, you grow to learn your partner's flaws. Now, before we get on to this topic, let's all just agree that every single fucking person in the entire world has at least one flaw about themselves. There is not a single hope or scientific element that'll make someone entirely flawless. It's fucking impossible. So yeah, Emily noticed my flaws. Snoring,

nose-picking, impressively long farting skill, high tolerance to whisky, etc.) and I discovered Emily's (Short-tempered psychopath, takes up 93 per cent of the bed, has more make-up in our room than a standard Sephora shop, etc.).

If you've an issue with someone's flaws but they're not interfering with the relationship, you have no choice but to accept them, understand them and live with them. You cannot change someone else and should never be selfish enough to. Unless you genuinely think it will better the person.

I need to make it clear to you that cheating, physical abuse or an aggressive and threatening attitude is NOT a flaw. I'm saying it's not a flaw because it's a serious fucking issue. To get off topic for a second and be serious: if you've ever experienced any of the issues, do not be afraid to talk to someone about it. No matter what gender you are. Hitting, mocking, cheating and belittling is fucking disgusting and you should leave the fucking asshole who does it to you.

FRIENDSHIP

When Emily and I became 'official', we became boyfriend and girlfriend, life partners, humans joined by love. Whatever the fuck you want to call it. When we were official I gained a girlfriend. In the first few months I gained not just a girlfriend, but also a best friend. There's nothing better than being able to have a best friend as a partner. I mean, I can touch her boobies AND play Ray-man on the Xbox. It's the fucking best; I feel most couples agree that your partner is your best fucking friend and nothing or no-one knows you better than your partner.

'I MEAN, I CAN TOUCH HER BOOBIES AND PLAY RAY-MAN ON THE XBOX. IT'S THE FUCKING BEST.'

AND LASTLY, SUCCESS

When Emily and I met each other, we had no idea that in two years' time, we'd accidentally create a company from the Internet. When we were first seeing each other, I had to sell my GoPro camera to some dude named Mark (shout out to you, Mark). I sold my cameras and that allowed me to get about four trips to see Emily.

We hadn't a penny to our names. I was living with 10€ in my pocket and she was earning 50€ a week working in a cloakroom in a nightclub.

After a time, she suggested videos to make, she inspired me to keep doing it, we made an online page that got 1,500,000,000 views. Yeah, that's 1.5 billion… in two years. We've focused on our future and set goals that we believe we'll achieve.

She told me to never give up, and I didn't. I went from having to sell my shit to get buses to see her to being in the Top 30 entrepreneurs under the age of 30 in Ireland. I'll never stop thanking her. We went from nothing to a little something and I'll forever be grateful.

WHEN YOU START TO GET BORED OF EACH OTHER...

I will say, it's okay to feel like you want to throw a plate at your partner's head at times, only you don't actually do it, of course. You'll experience great moments and you'll experience completely disastrous moments.

Let's start with the good, shall we? If you want my honest advice, travel as much as you possibly can, whether it be a trip to Cuba or even a simple bus adventure. The more things you do the better, especially when you're young. It's a great way of spending time together and creating memories. Don't waste time on Netflix and not talking to each other doing the same shit every day; go out and enjoy each other while enjoying the world. Now let's talk about the bad parts of spending time together.

If you're just both sitting there on your phones pointlessly scrolling through Instagram and Facebook you're bound to get a little bored of each other. I mean, you're both literally two boring fucks who are sitting on a couch saying or doing nothing, of course you're going to want to kill each other. It's totally fucking normal. But do try to avoid it. Yes, people are entitled to just sit there and do nothing all day, I do it all the time. But I still prioritise my little adventures with Emily.

'I MEAN, YOU'RE BOTH LITERALLY TWO BORING FUCKS WHO ARE SITTING ON A COUCH SAYING OR DOING NOTHING, OF COURSE YOU'RE GOING TO WANT TO KILL EACH OTHER.'

EMILY'S VERSION

Ladies, when watching Netflix, there's nothing more satisfying than having total control over what we watch. I usually watch 13 Reasons Why, Pretty Little Liars, Grey's Anatomy and pretty much anything else that only I enjoy. If your partner tells you to change it to something that he or she can enjoy, just simply tell them to go into the bedroom, light a few candles, turn on some smooth jazz, close the curtains and dim the lights so they can romantically go fuck themselves.

'TELL YOUR PARTNER TO GO INTO THE BEDROOM, LIGHT A FEW CANDLES, TURN ON SOME SMOOTH JAZZ, CLOSE THE CURTAINS AND DIM THE LIGHTS SO THEY CAN ROMANTICALLY GO FUCK THEMSELVES.'

If you're worried about you getting bored of your partner or your partner getting bored of you... Well, I have a simple solution for you. Here are some examples from personal experience that you can learn from:

If your partner says you're boring, tell him to go off and date some bitch that's exciting then, cos he won't find her here.

If your partner says he's losing interest in you, tell him that when he leaves he's going to regret seeing my bomb ass selfie pictures on Instagram in six months.

And lastly, if your partner says you're crazy, beat him with a soft object, such as a sock full of batteries or even a pillow case filled with eyeshadow palettes, either one will do the job. Trust a bitch on this one.

CIAN v EMILY

Cian

Emily, you do realise that you've just publicly announced that you physically abuse me with hard objects?

Emily

Ah, but it's harmless, babe. If a dog pees on the carpet you tap him on the nose. And if you call me crazy I'll beat you to death with your own footwear.

Cian

You can't just do that to me, Emily. You're making me go off topic again, but babe, you totally made me look like the bad guy in your advice section.

Emily

Emily: Yeah yeah yeah. Cry me a fucking river, sweetheart.

Cian

You're fucking crazy, you know that?

Emily

Oh, sweetie, you better start running because I'm taking my sock off and I'm getting fucking golf balls from the cabinet.

'OH, SWEETIE, YOU BETTER START RUNNING BECAUSE I'M TAKING MY SOCK OFF AND I'M GETTING FUCKING GOLF BALLS FROM THE CABINET.'

THE REAL STORY

So the real story here is quite complicated. Because whenever you, the viewer, see lovely and cute photos or videos of Emily and I on Facebook, Snapchat or Instagram, you'll also see us often referred to as 'couple goals' or 'relationship goals'. But to be quite honest, our relationship isn't perfect. And I'm grateful for it. We argue all the time, sometimes for stupid reasons and sometimes for more serious reasons. Because we work from home, we're in each other's faces 24/7. We're bound to take stress out on each other – who else is going to! Emily and I know that no matter how loud and foul our arguments get, they always end with a kiss on the forehead and a tear-soaked shoulder from Emily resting her head on me. Arguments heal things, they fix a problem. Usually arguments are necessary because you can't treat your relationship like a glass jar and fill it with compressed air. It'll eventually blow into pieces from not leaving it out.

Emily and I found it a little difficult trying to do things together at first. The main reason is because we hate people, socialising, nightclubs and restaurants. We enjoy being in the middle of fucking nowhere being the two little weirdos that we are without a care in the world. Sometimes we go on road trips to a beach 300 miles away, stay there for 20 minutes and then head home again. There's nothing better than a day well spent with your partner, just out of the house with your phone on silent and enjoying each other's company.

'WE ENJOY BEING IN THE MIDDLE OF FUCKING NOWHERE BEING THE TWO LITTLE WEIRDOS THAT WE ARE WITHOUT A CARE IN THE WORLD.'

WHERE WERE WE LIVING?

When you're in a relationship, it's important to take your steps nice and slow. Sometimes people tend to rush into things prematurely without thinking of the consequences. Let time do its job and go with the flow. If whatever happens will happen, there is absolutely no reason to rush it. Moving into a home together is a huge step in a relationship. Sometimes this wouldn't be necessary for a few months into the relationship with the exception of long-distance relationships. You're taking a risk when rushing into moving in together. Some people think they get on great but they don't realise that they only see each other for a very small percentage of the week. When they move in together they may discover that they have a short fuse when it comes to the other partner, causing some unnecessary bullshit arguments that waste precious energy that could be spent on chewing pasta. But hey! Sometimes it works out perfectly fine and when the couple move in together they get on like a house on fire. Not literally a house on fire. I hope you realise that I was just using a common expression that symbolises two humans interacting peacefully and positively with no issues... ah, whatever.

EMILY'S VERSION

It pissed me off whenever Cian came over to my house and dragged his big praying mantis-looking feet around my fake polar bear rug. I mean, I don't blame a bitch for getting irritated when her man comes all up in her home thinking he owns the place with his big crustaceous feet. Get the fuck outta here, mista.

If you want my honest advice, ladies, let the fucker wait for months, maybe even a year! If you move in together, he's gonna spend 80 per cent of the time trying to feel your booty and burp his ABCs — you don't need that in your life just yet, sweetie.

Another thing you don't appreciate until you move in together is freedom. I can't even fuck off to have a booty bomb in the toilet without Cian asking me where I'm going. I'm going for a fucking shit, Cian, okay? Is that fucking okay with you? What are you? The fucking CIA with all of your interrogation questions? Let a gal drop a log in peace, thank you very much.

To conclude my perfect and detailed advice, let him wait. Make sure he's into it to swim lengths, not just in for a quick dip. You ain't no booty call, you the main booty and the only bootie. He's gonna be waiting.

'YOU AIN'T NO BOOTY CALL, YOU THE MAIN BOOTY AND THE ONLY BOOTIE. HE'S GONNA BE WAITING.'

CIAN v EMILY

EMILY, WHY DID YOU EVEN MENTION THE TIMES WHEN I ASK YOU IF YOU'RE GOING FOR A POO? THAT'S SO DISRESPECTFUL TO MY PRIVACY!

AH, PIPE DOWN YA FUCKEN WHINGEBAG. HAVE YOU ANYTHING BETTER TO BE DOING THAN COMPLAINING LIKE YOU'RE MOANING FUCKING MYRTLE?

ALL I'M SAYING IS, YOU'RE GIVING FUCKING SHIT ADVICE YET AGAIN AND I FEEL YOU MIGHT HAVE TO STOP CONTRIBUTING TO MY BOOK.

OKAY, SWEETIE, DO YOU SEE THAT HAMMER OVER THERE?

YEAH?

DO YOU KNOW THAT I WOULD LOVE TO SMASH YOUR KNEE CAPS IN WITH IT?

EMILY, THAT'S A BIT FUCKING ABUSIVE, DON'T DO THAT TO ME.

OH HERE WE GO AGAIN, WHINGEING AS USUAL!

THE REAL STORY

Moving in together should be a well-thought-out and perfectly planned process. It shouldn't be a spur-of-the-moment decision. Now, I'm being a total hypocrite here by going against my own advice as Emily moved into my mother's house where I was living after I had known her for only seven months. Our excuse was the long distance was too expensive so it would have made more sense to move Emily into my tiny bedroom in my mother's house. My darling angel of a mother, Liz, opened her arms to Emily like she was one of her own. I forever thank her for helping our relationship become so much more real. After time went on Emily and I started hating each other, ha ha, seriously. We were cooped up in a small room meant for one person, and it only had one wardrobe so our clothes were literally covering every part of the ground, you couldn't see the wood flooring. If you watch my old videos you'll know the room that I'm talking about. As time went on, we decided enough was enough and we got our own place.

Emily and I were going for a really nice and luxurious apartment. Luckily because we both made a comfortable living from the videos and other platforms, we managed to get a penthouse suite. Not to be showing off or to be materialistic, it was more of a motivator for me. I earned every square inch of that penthouse and all it can do is motivate me to work even harder. All I gotta do is believe in myself; this time last year I couldn't afford a large Big Mac meal.

WHEN YOU START TO REALLY GET TO KNOW EACH OTHER...

Getting to know each other is pretty simple. You sit down, leave your phones in another room, light a candle and ask each other every single possible question that you could think of, whether it be if they prefer spaghetti Bolognese or spaghetti carbonara or another question as equally important as that. You could also ask the things that you need to know, such as 'Have you ever killed somebody?' and 'Have you a substantial history in cheating?' Or even 'Are you going to make my life a complete and utter misery?' If you want to have a healthy relationship, you need to have an honest relationship. Don't have any skeletons or lies buried deep in your closet.

Habits are things you learn as the relationship progresses. Some people dislike their partner's habits, whereas other people simply ignore their habits. But most people fucking hate it. You can never have a good habit, really, can you? It's not like you develop a habit for cleaning the house and ensuring it's spotless. ALL HABITS ARE FUCKING ANNOYING. Whether it's nail-biting, smoking, hair-playing, farting, burping or even spitting (not that kind, you fucking disgusting-minded freak).

Couples tend to help each other with their bad and nasty habits. For example, I'm sure a FUCK LOAD of people quit smoking cigarettes for the sake of their happiness in the relationship. Habits can sometimes create tiny sub-arguments that are stupid and unnecessary. Nip the habits in the bud, before it's too late.

'ALL HABITS ARE FUCKING ANNOYING. WHETHER IT'S NAIL-BITING, SMOKING, HAIR-PLAYING, FARTING, BURPING OR EVEN SPITTING (NOT THAT KIND YOU FUCKING DISGUSTING MINDED FREAK).'

EMILY'S VERSION

Y'know, ladies, my man Cian always decides to chastise and mortify me in public whenever my habits kick in. I mean, It's not my fault that my habits include bitching at girls who look at my boyfriend, walking into every possible clothes shop in sight but purchasing nothing, grabbing my boyfriend's booty whenever I catch a bitch staring just so she knows that I own his fat ass. In my opinion, if he can't handle the heat, tell him to get out of the kitchen, cos you shouldn't have to change for nobody. If you smoke 20 cigarettes a day and he tells you to quit, smoke 40 cigarettes a day. Fuck that asshole, he's nothing but a prick. I've always been passionate when it comes to being independent and if I want to play the Nintendo Wii at 4 a.m. when everyone is asleep then so be it! I don't need no man comin' all up in my business and leisure time. I sometimes even pretend to go for a poo but I'm playing Nintendo Dogs on the Nintendo DS, he never suspects a thing. So there's a bit of advice, if you want to hide your bad habits, you're best to do them when you're in the toilet pretending to take a shit.

'I'VE ALWAYS BEEN PASSIONATE WHEN IT COMES TO BEING INDEPENDENT AND IF I WANT TO PLAY THE NINTENDO WII AT 4 A.M. WHEN EVERYONE IS ASLEEP THEN SO BE IT!'

CIAN v EMILY

EMILY, THAT WAS POTENTIALLY THE WORST POSSIBLE ADVICE I'VE EVER READ IN MY ENTIRE LIFE. WHAT THE FUCK HAS GOTTEN INTO YOU?

WELL, CIAN, MAYBE I'M JUST FUCKEN SICK OF LISTENING TO YOUR SHIT.

DOES THAT HAVE ANYTHING TO DO WITH YOUR LACK OF GOOD CONTENT FOR THIS BOOK? YEAH?

LIKE I SAID, SWEET PEA, I'M SICK OF LISTENING TO YOUR BORING-ASS ADVICE. I'D RATHER PAINT MY ENTIRE BODY WITH NAIL VARNISH INSTEAD OF READING YOUR FUCKING DREADFUL ADVICE.

YOU... YOU THINK MY ADVICE IS DREADFUL?

WELL, LET'S PUT IT TO THE TEST... SO Y'KNOW IF HYPOTHETICALLY I WANTED TO ASK YOU TO BUY ME A NEW HANDBAG, WHAT WOULD YOU SAY?

I'D SAY YOU NEED TO EARN THAT REWARD BECAUSE—

BORING, SHUT THE FUCK UPPPPPP.

'I'D RATHER PAINT MY ENTIRE BODY WITH NAIL VARNISH INSTEAD OF READING YOUR FUCKING DREADFUL ADVICE.'

THE REAL STORY

Emily and I didn't really talk about any of our bad habits until we discovered them by ourselves. A good example of that would be that Emily didn't know I smoked until one month of knowing me. She discovered the night she met me in person as I sparked up an Amber Leaf rollie. Luckily, Emily helped me quit smoking cigarettes, I still thank her to this day, nearly two years now since I last had a cigarette.

We got to know each other quite fast, as all we were doing was spending time together 24/7! She learned that I have a few habits, which included the habit of saying 'fucking' in every sentence. It wasn't my fault, I'm fucking working on it, okay?

Emily had no real habits. One that I'm discovering recently is her habit of nail-biting. Usually Emily has these big fancy-ass nails that look like a professional artist spent hours creating these abstract masterpieces that are then semi-permanently stuck to your fingers for a month or so. One of Emily's fancy nails got caught in the fridge door and snapped off, causing Emily to lose it. She ended up biting all of them off one by one. And now all she does is bites her nails down to the fucking bottom. Horrible little gremlin she is.

'SHE LEARNED THAT I HAVE A FEW HABITS, WHICH INCLUDED THE HABIT OF SAYING "FUCKING" IN EVERY SENTENCE I WOULD SAY. IT WASN'T MY FAULT, I'M FUCKING WORKING ON IT OKAY?'

WHEN YOU BEGIN TO DABBLE IN PDA POLITICS...

Before we get started with this, let me just briefly explain what a PDA is. PDA is 'Public Display of Affection', that is, when a couple does fucking horrible things in public such as holding hands and even kissing, how fucking dare they.

I don't quite know if I should give advice about how to use PDA in your relationship or how to fucking avoid the disgusting shit.

Okay, so let's create a scenario here. You and your girlfriend are at a bus stop. You're not getting on the bus, she is. You're waiting there with her because you're a great fucking guy. Out of nowhere the bus arrives, and people form a queue to board the bus. Your girlfriend looks at you and says, 'Oh look, it's time to go' and she leans in for a kiss. Your heart starts racing, people start staring. 'Is he going to be that fucking disgusting and really kiss his girlfriend in PUBLIC?!' I should fucking hope not.

As she's going in for the kiss, strategically place a slice of warm ham between her lips and your lips. People will accuse you of PDA, but in reality you're just feeding your girlfriend ham. It's a win–win, take my advice.

'PEOPLE WILL ACCUSE YOU OF PDA, BUT IN REALITY YOU'RE JUST FEEDING YOUR GIRLFRIEND HAM.'

EMILY'S VERSION

Heartbreak, illness, poverty, disease, addiction, crisis, hunger. You know what all of these things have in common? They are all not as bad as seeing two fucking rodents kissing in public. Oh Christ all-fucking-mighty, every day before I leave for the boutique that I get my nails done in I pray that I don't see anyone holding hands, hugging, kissing or even flirting in public. It makes me want to vomit violently everywhere.

If you're a person who contributes to public display of affection, I suggest you fucking stop or I will have to take action similar to when they were burning witches. Yeah, motherfucker, I ain't fucking around, you hear me? DO YOU?

But in all seriousness, I do crave Cian's hand when I lead him round Sephora trying to find the new Kat Von D eyeshadow palettes. I don't know if I crave affection when holding his hand, or it's just similar to having your dog on a leash. You don't want him running off and humping some other bitch in a field by the bench now, do you? Hell naw! Fuck that, big boy.

CIAN v EMILY

EMILY, DID YOU JUST COMPARE A HUMAN RELATIONSHIP
TO DOGS HUMPING IN THE LOCAL PARK?

Y'KNOW WHAT, CIAN? YES. YES I FUCKEN DID.

OKAY, WELL, I DON'T THINK IT'S QUITE APPROPRIATE. I MEAN,
YOU COMPARED DISEASE AND ADDICTION TO PUBLIC DISPLAY OF
AFFECTION. DO YOU NOT THINK THAT'S A LITTLE TOO MUCH?

JESUS, CIAN, YOU REALLY DO WORRY A LOT, DON'T YOU?

WELL YEAH, EMILY. I MEAN, PEOPLE ARE GOING
TO BE READING THIS BOOK AND THINK WE'RE
COMPLETELY UNPROFESSIONAL.

CIAN, DARLING, LET'S BE REALISTIC. THE ONLY
PERSON THAT'S GOING TO ACTUALLY READ THIS FAR
INTO THE BOOK IS YOUR MOTHER. HI, MOMMA LIZ!

MOM, STOP READING THIS PART. IT'S ABOUT
TO GET NASTY. FUCK YOU, EMILY.

GASP HOW FUCKING DARE YOU, MISTER, YOU JUST
SAID THAT WHILE YOUR MOTHER READS YOUR FAKE
ARGUMENT BETWEEN YOU AND YOUR ALTER EGO.

YOU'RE STARTING TO CONFUSE ME, EMILY.

YEAH, WELL, YOU'RE THE ONE TYPING THIS.

'THE ONLY PERSON THAT'S GOING TO ACTUALLY READ THIS FAR INTO THE BOOK IS YOUR MOTHER. HI, MOMMA LIZ!'

THE REAL STORY

Emily and I are pretty anti-PDA. We don't hold hands, we don't kiss and we don't even hug in public. Don't get me wrong, I mean, we love each other very much, but it doesn't mean we have to shove our tongues down our mouths in the middle of a restaurant. I don't need to express my love to Emily by kissing her neck on a public bus.

Yes, we may hold hands on the very odd occasion, but that's just simple tradition. If you think about it, it's kind of weird. I mean, two mammals constantly holding each other's limbs in fear of separating while walking around Lush Cosmetics, smelling bath bombs and lip scrubs.

We keep our affection at home. There, I kiss her all the time. I hug her before I venture off to the toilet to take a shit. I cuddle her when we watch *Spongebob* and sometimes even touch her bum.

When we're travelling we like to people watch in cafes to see the different mentality the locals have. For example, we noticed Amsterdam and Paris had the most number of PDAs. We saw this couple on the Métro in Paris practically eating each other's faces off in an attempt to kiss each other. Save it for home, Pierre.

'WE KEEP OUR AFFECTION AT HOME; I KISS HER ALL THE TIME. I HUG HER BEFORE I VENTURE OFF TO THE TOILET TO TAKE A SHIT. I CUDDLE HER WHEN WE WATCH *SPONGEBOB* AND SOMETIMES EVEN TOUCH HER BUM.'

WHEN YOU'D LIKE TO SAY 'I LOVE YOU'...
CIAN'S VERSION

I'm going to try and give my best potential advice from both a) planning on when to first say it and b) how to react when it's first said to you.

Now, let's start with how to plan it. First things first, my dudes, you need to make sure you actually love the person before you admit it to them. Because, well, if you tell a girl or guy you love them and you end up not loving them and leaving, you have no fucking idea how much you have just hurt that person, you thick and dense motherfucker. But if you're certain you love your partner, take a deep-ass breath because trust me you're going to be fucking nervous, man! But it's okay, it's normal. Try to translate it to excitement and pray she loves you back!

Also make sure you find a good setting for when you're going to say it. I mean, you don't want to say something like that on a bus or something. Unless the bus is empty, which is totally fine. Or the bus is full of lovely people, which isn't beyond the realms of possibility. But be prepared for their reaction when you do say it. Setting, for containing said reaction, is therefore pretty key...

When someone says, 'I love you' it can be a lot to take in, you could even go into shock, who knows?!

First, if someone admits their feelings to you, you should be very fucking grateful that someone somehow finds you attractive. Second, don't just stand there like a goat looking at thunder and lightning in the mountains. If you love the person back, just fucking say it. Embrace it, don't be like, 'Aww thanks but I'm not ready for commitment', oh fuck off, you stubborn cow.

And what happens if they don't say, 'I love you' back? Well, you can pretend you didn't say it. Or pretend you said it by accident; like it was a sneeze or something. Or that you were talking to someone else. Or simply ask them: why? and then begin to weep uncontrollably...

EMILY'S VERSION

Boys come up to me all the time and are like, 'Oh my God, Emily, I'm so in love with you, you're fucking sexy, can I grab your digits?' and I'm always like, 'Nah, bitch, I got a hubby, so fuck off back under the rock you crawled out of, you creep.' Sometimes people think I'm being rude but I'm just being silly ole me defending myself from any strangers.

When Cian said he loved me it was just before my burritos kicked in. As soon as he said it I let out a large cheek squeak. He looked confused and I went white in the face while he choked on my Mexican massacre fart.

If a man says he loves you, don't say, 'I love you too' unless you've given him a credit check and make sure he's got a hell of a lot of money. I mean, c'mon sweetie, I can't love a chubby-bearded guy unless he's got enough in the bank to get me a Gucci purse. Ahhh, love is great, isn't it?

'IF A MAN SAYS HE LOVES YOU, DON'T SAY,
'I LOVE YOU TOO' UNLESS YOU'VE GIVEN HIM
A CREDIT CHECK AND MAKE SURE HE'S GOT
A HELL OF A LOT OF MONEY.'

CIAN v EMILY

Cian

Why do you keep thinking that I have money, Emily?

Emily

Because you do, Cian.

Cian

Emily, I have no more than any other average 22-year-old.

Emily

Well, where did you get the money for that Louis Vuitton suitcase you got me?

Cian

I worked overtime for six months to afford it.

Emily

Oh... and what about my Fenti flip-flops?

Cian

I used my birthday money to buy you them so I could apologise to you for when you ate my food and then hit me.

Emily

Oh yeah, you did, ah ha. So you don't have money?

Cian

No, babe, ha ha. Not as much as you think, anyway.

Emily

Oh, right. Okay, so yeah it was lovely knowing you.

Cian

What? Where are you going?

Emily

Ah, just for some milk. See you ehm... soon or something.

THE REAL STORY

The real story of how Emily and I first admitted we loved each other is not as romantic as you would think. It all started back in February 2015. Emily and I were just about a couple. We weren't official, but we were most definitely 'exclusive' to each other. Emily was in Waterford and I was in Cork. She was out having a few drinks with her friends. I was out with my friend Kevin when I got a text message from Emily saying something along the lines of, 'Hey Cian, I just wanted to text you to say that I love you, you're just so amazing and blah blah blah'.

Now as I was reading that text I was smoking a cigarette while listening to A Tribe Called Quest with Kevin. And she was in some sweaty-ass nightclub intoxicated by horrible and overpriced alcohol that she regretted having drunk in the morning.

That's probably the least romantic story you've heard about two people admitting that they love each other. Shame. Sighhhhhhh.

WHEN YOU JUST HAVE TO GO...

CIAN'S VERSION

Ahhhh, the ole first fart, something that'll set you up for a fun and stinky relationship. Farting and going to the toilet in front of your partner is a challenge that everyone in a relationship will face. It's going to happen, people, it's inevitable. When you're on your first date, most people think about the future and what she'll look like in her wedding dress or something. But me? I'll just stare at her thinking, 'I'm going to be taking a shit in front of you someday down the line.'

Farting and pooping is fucking normal, people. It happens. Beyoncé, Queen Elizabeth, your own grandmother, even Ellen DeGeneres has to go.

They all fart and they all poo, now has that comforted you a little? If you're worrying about farting or pooping in front of your partner, just make a joke out of it. If he freaks out, you've got yourself a fucking loser. If he laughs and joins you by shitting in the bath tub, you've got yourself a creep. But if you have a guy that'll laugh at it, you've got yourself a keeper. In a nutshell, just be yourself. If you fart during movies, just do it anyway. If you have someone who doesn't agree or like it, tell him to grow the fuck up and have a nap.

'I'LL JUST STARE AT HER THINKING, 'I'M GOING TO BE TAKING A SHIT IN FRONT OF YOU SOMEDAY DOWN THE LINE.'

EMILY'S VERSION

Ladies, let me say this as clear and simply as possible. If you ever fart or poop in front of your boyfriend, you're in for a real disaster. I once heard that in Rome, Italy during the 1300s, a woman left out a booty bomb by accident during her marriage. When the groom heard her fart, he covered his nose, walked out the house and married her sister instead. So devastating. If only she didn't let off a bum burp. She'd be married with kids, but now she's just a pasta maker for an Italian gang in north Nebraska.

If you need to fart, I would definitely suggest shouting for no reason to mask the sound of the booty bomb. When your partner asks what's wrong, you can just say that someone unfollowed you on Twitter or something, but in reality you're just letting a few pieces of smell out into the atmosphere.

On the occasion, that you have to hide your trips to the toilet (not that it happens very often with us), usually I just run a bath because my poops last fucken years. Was that a little too much information? Ah well get over it, you should have fucken expected it.

CIAN v EMILY

Cian

So you're trying to tell me that every time you go for a bath, you're just taking a shit?

Emily

Ah ha, yeahhhhh. It's something I've been hiding for quite some time now.

Cian

Emily, babe, you do realise that it's okay to shit.

Emily

Eh? Cian, you do realise that that's fucking disgusting.

Cian

I know, babe, but I'm just letting you know that it's okay to poo.

Emily

I know it's okay, babe, but my poops are not to be showcased.

Cian

Why?

Emily

Because I'm sure there's something dead in there?

Cian

In where?

Emily

...in my bum.

Cian

Emily this is getting so fucking weird.

Emily

Yeah let's watch *Pretty Little Liars* and forget about all of this. But first, I'm going to go and have a bath.......

THE REAL STORY

Okay so before we get this started, I just need for you to be aware that I'm a very open person. I think you've realised this already, but I don't know if many people talk about their moments on the toilet. Or, to say it as it is, shitting.

This story sounds funny but I was being serious at the time, so do try to understand my attempt of being serious. Ladies, y'know the way you have tests or tricks to find out what kind of man your guy is, well, us guys have tests too. For example, the first time that Emily met me is the first time she heard me fart. We were in the car and I just let one peep out. It wasn't to laugh about and be disgusting, it was more of a test to see how she'd handle the situation. As soon as she heard my fart perfectly produced in the note of E major, her eyes lit up as they opened followed by a smirk with a gentle head nod. She commended my efforts, she even graded it a Grade A fart. Two years later, here we are, in love and shitting in front of each other with the door open. It's real romantic.

'WE WERE IN THE CAR AND I JUST LET ONE PEEP OUT.'

WHEN IT'S YOUR FIRST ANNIVERSARY...

CIAN'S VERSION

Forget about the first week anniversaries or even the first month anniversaries. It's all about the 1st year anniversary. Congratulations, you've successfully survived an entire year with a fucking psychopath.

Now it's pretty natural for the woman to show more interest and participation when it comes to that majestic day. Usually it's dinner, flowers and a gift.

When it comes to the anniversary date, you should most definitely prepare for it. Don't be a last-minute person who ends up getting a shitty-ass gift.

I also need to stress that not everyone are 'gifting' couples and that's totally fucking normal. But this is my book and I'll write whatever the fuck I want in it so have a Coke, smile, and shut the fuck up.

A woman cannot resist a dozen roses, chocolates and a teddy bear. But I need to stress that they don't mean shit if you aren't treating her the way she should be treated, and the same comes from the opposite side. It's pointless being half-hearted all year then buying a €6 card from Hallmark thinking it'll make up for all of it. But considering you've made it to your year anniversary, I can imagine you're doing a good job so give yourself a pat on the back, champ.

EMILY'S VERSION

Okay, ladies, the year is closing and your year anniversary is coming closer by the day. You have your dress purchased, your fake tan applied and you even went off to get your nails done and individual eyelashes put on. You head home to do your make-up and BOOM! He's forgotten and is heading to the bar with the boys.

If this or something similar happens, you need to round up all of your girlfriends from north, south, east and west so you can triangulate his location using make-up pallets and pictures of puppies. I can't guarantee it works all the time, but for me it does so you can't say my advice is bullshit, okay bitch?

My idea of a perfect night for an anniversary is Netflix, sweet and sour chicken, shaved legs and no pants. No, not for any sexy things, you pervert, what kind of book do you think this fucking is, you creep? How many times do I have to fucken warn you?

If he hasn't gotten you any gift, just use it against him for future arguements. That's what I do all the time. For example, when Cian's great-aunt died I didn't want to go to the funeral. He gave out to me for not going but was it as bad as never getting me a fucking present for our anniversary? Fuck you and your great-aunt, Cian darling.

CIAN v EMILY

I BOUGHT YOU A FUCKING PONY FOR OUR ANNIVERSARY AND I TOOK YOU TO PARIS!

OH. I THOUGHT THAT THEY WERE JUST RANDOM GIFTS, AH HA.

EMILY, YOU CAN'T JUST WRITE THAT AFTER ME BEING SO NICE TO YOU.

OH BOO FUCKING HOO. GIVE ME A BREAK, DARLING. YOU'RE JUST PISSED OFF THAT PEOPLE THINK YOU'RE HORRIBLE.

YEAH I AM, EMILY! BECAUSE I'M NOT ∧ BAD AS YOU MAKE ME OUT TO BE.

I'M SORRY, IS THIS THE SAME PERSON THAT MAKES FUCKING VIDEOS ABOUT HIS GIRLFRIEND MAKING HER OUT TO BE A PSYCHOPATH?!

YEAH, THAT'S DIFFERENT, EMILY. PEOPLE KNOW THAT I'M JOKING.

THEY KNOW YOU'RE JOKING, AND NOW THEY KNOW THAT YOU NEVER GOT ME A GIFT.

I GOT YOU A FUCKING PONY AND A TRIP TO PARIS.

YEAH BUT THAT WASN'T ON THE FUCKING DAY OF OUR ANNIVERSARY SO IT DOESN'T FUCKING COUNT, YOU PRICK.

THE REAL STORY

For our first-year anniversary I gave Emily a letter that contained the booking confirmation for Paris. We left two days after. Paris was cool, a little bit smelly and some of the locals refused to speak English. Lol, okay, French lady, if you don't want to sell me some of your sandwiches, I'll just fuck off to the other store to someone who actually cares about the tourists, mainly because they're FUCKING CUSTOMERS! What are you? A goddamn money-hater?

I also gave her Emily jar containing 365 letters that she will open once a day. That jar had 365 reasons why I love her.

Basically, make your girl happy. Go on to Tumblr or Pinterest to find cute ass ideas, you'll never fail from there!

'I ALSO GAVE HER A JAR CONTAINING 365 LETTERS THAT SHE WILL OPEN ONCE A DAY. THAT JAR HAD 365 REASONS WHY I LOVE HER.'

THE CIAN AND EMILY Q&A — PART TWO

WHAT'S THE BEST THING ABOUT LIFE?

CIAN

I think being able to share life with another person is truly amazing!

EMILY

Discount codes. Yeah, definitely discount codes.

IF YOU GOT STRANDED ON AN ISLAND, WHAT WOULD YOU HAVE WITH YOU IF YOU ONLY HAD ONE CHOICE?

CIAN

I think I would have to have a source of nutrients so I could survive long enough to plan how to leave the island safely and efficiently to ensure I can make the distance.

EMILY

Emmmm, I think I'd bring my hair curler because if there's anyone cute around I gotta be lookin' fine as hell.

WHAT IS THE HARDEST THING IN LIFE?

CIAN

Saying goodbye to a loved one who has passed.

EMILY

When you think you have another pack of crisps but you accidentally ate the last packet last night.

PART 3
MOVING IN

WHEN YOU NEED TO MEET THE IN-LAWS...

One of the scariest things for any man is to meet his partner's parents. It's that very moment when you walk through the door to see both the parents sitting there with a slight grin on their faces before asking you to sit and join them for some biscuits and tea. Yup, it's time for a good ole chat.

Now, advice for the gentlemen. I'm beyond confident with this subject and I do feel that what I say would work. If you're in love with this girl, it's not gonna happen if the parents aren't impressed. Whether you're 18 or 45, you'll always need permission from her parents. So, gentlemen, when you approach the mother, give her a kiss on the cheek followed by a hug and tell her she's beautiful or some shit. Works like a fucking charm.

Now once you're done flattering the mother, it's time for you to relax. I say 'relax' because you'll need your nerves to fuck off for this. You need to face the biggest challenge yet: it's time to meet your girlfriend's father. Now, trust me when I fucking say this, people, approach him with confidence, look him dead in the eye and when he sticks his hand out for you to shake, you'd better grab that hand harder than a fucking crocodile does with a zebra. You better cause some motherfucking blood loss to his fingertips to impress this prick. Tell him he has fantastic hair, offer him a two-week golf trip to Scotland and boom! You're in the fucking family.

'TELL HIM HE HAS FANTASTIC HAIR, OFFER HIM A TWO-WEEK GOLF TRIP TO SCOTLAND AND BOOM! YOU'RE IN THE FUCKING FAMILY.'

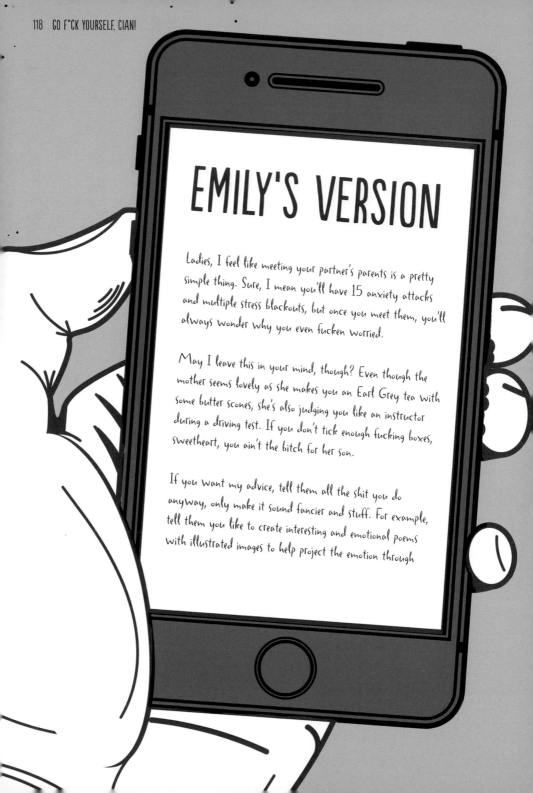

EMILY'S VERSION

Ladies, I feel like meeting your partner's parents is a pretty simple thing. Sure, I mean you'll have 15 anxiety attacks and multiple stress blackouts, but once you meet them, you'll always wonder why you even fucken worried.

May I leave this in your mind, though? Even though the mother seems lovely as she makes you an Earl Grey tea with some butter scones, she's also judging you like an instructor during a driving test. If you don't tick enough fucking boxes, sweetheart, you ain't the bitch for her son.

If you want my advice, tell them all the shit you do anyway, only make it sound fancier and stuff. For example, tell them you like to create interesting and emotional poems with illustrated images to help project the emotion through

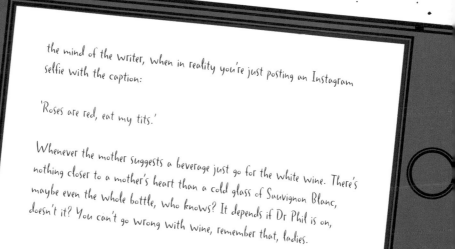

the mind of the writer, when in reality you're just posting an Instagram selfie with the caption:

'Roses are red, eat my tits.'

Whenever the mother suggests a beverage just go for the white wine. There's nothing closer to a mother's heart than a cold glass of Sauvignon Blanc, maybe even the whole bottle, who knows? It depends if Dr Phil is on, doesn't it? You can't go wrong with wine, remember that, ladies.

'IF YOU DON'T TICK ENOUGH FUCKING BOXES SWEETHEART, YOU AIN'T THE BITCH FOR MY SON.'

CIAN v EMILY

EMILY, HOW COME I HAVEN'T MET YOUR PARENTS YET?

BECAUSE, CIAN, I'M JUST A FICTIONAL CHARACTER INVENTED BY YOU. MY PARENTS ARE TECHNICALLY YOU.

WHOA, I'VE NEVER THOUGHT ABOUT THAT. SO LIKE... ARE YOU MY GIRLFRIEND OR MY DAUGHTER?

I'M EHHHHH... I DON'T... I DON'T FUCKEN KNOW ACTUALLY.

WELL, TECHNICALLY YOU'RE JUST MY ALTER EGO, SO YOU'RE NOTHING ELSE.

SO IS THAT ALL I AM TO YOU? JUST SOME SHITTY CHARACTER YOU CREATED FOR COMEDIC ENTERTAINMENT?

WELL, YEAH. I MEAN.... WHAT ELSE ARE YOU HERE FOR?

I TRULY HOPE YOU DIE SLOWLY, CIAN.

THE REAL STORY

So, the real story about how we met each other's parents is pretty simple. Let's start off with Emily meeting my parents. Now before we start it off, Emily got lucky with me as she only had to deal with the pressure of meeting one of my parents because my father is not exactly alive right now. Yes, I know that sounds disrespectful, but you haven't seen fucking anything yet.

When Emily met my mother it was not a big deal. In fact, it wasn't planned in the slightest. Emily was just in my house one day when my mother came home with the shopping. I suggested we both go downstairs and help her out by bringing in the grocery bags. She hesitated but agreed. When we came down my mother was like, 'Oh, hello there' and I said, 'Mom I'd like for you to meet Emily' and then they talked about make-up and shit so that's literally all it was.

I met Emily's father and mother at two separate times. In fact, I met Emily's mother and two brothers before I met her father. Her mother, Lindy, is your stereotypical mother. Caring, loving and makes infinite sandwiches and cups of tea. Her brothers, Shane and Dean, were at first slightly intimidating as they're both over six foot and hard and shit and I'm a chubby five foot seven dude with a pair of Vans on. After we got to know each other we all figured out that we would get on just fine. Everyone was hyping Seamie up to being the scary father who would batter you into a dimension of terror and chaos, so I was petrified to meet him. My hands were sweating so much that I needed tissue to dry them (see chapter 'What to do with my Sweaty Hands' for more advice on this). All of a sudden, the car pulls up into the drive, the keys are in the door, followed by heavy footsteps. My heart was pounding until boom, Seamie enters the room. He shook my hand and I grabbed that motherfucker like it was the last chicken nugget on the plate and the whole family wanted it.

They now treat me like I'm a son of their own and the brothers are considered my brothers too. It's weird having a second family. Thank fuck they like me.

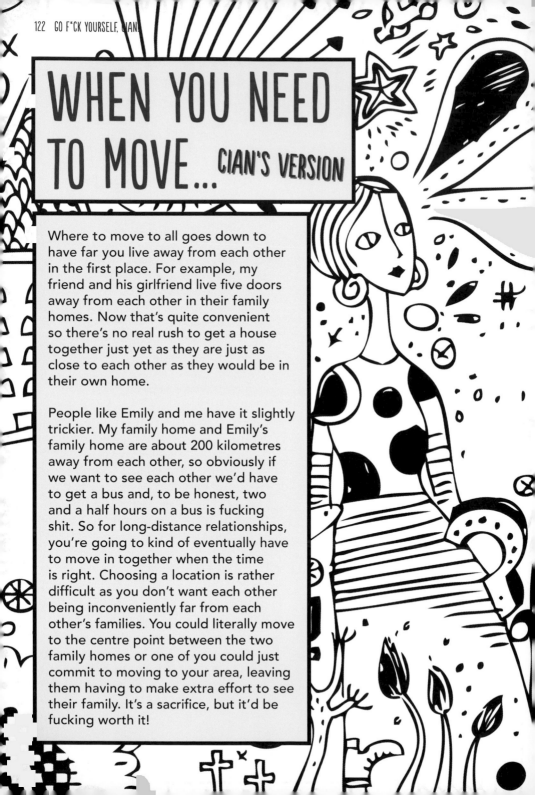

WHEN YOU NEED TO MOVE... CIAN'S VERSION

Where to move to all goes down to have far you live away from each other in the first place. For example, my friend and his girlfriend live five doors away from each other in their family homes. Now that's quite convenient so there's no real rush to get a house together just yet as they are just as close to each other as they would be in their own home.

People like Emily and me have it slightly trickier. My family home and Emily's family home are about 200 kilometres away from each other, so obviously if we want to see each other we'd have to get a bus and, to be honest, two and a half hours on a bus is fucking shit. So for long-distance relationships, you're going to kind of eventually have to move in together when the time is right. Choosing a location is rather difficult as you don't want each other being inconveniently far from each other's families. You could literally move to the centre point between the two family homes or one of you could just commit to moving to your area, leaving them having to make extra effort to see their family. It's a sacrifice, but it'd be fucking worth it!

EMILY'S VERSION

Ladies, if you want to move in with your man or woman lover, you'd best remember that if it's an effort for you, fuck it. Of course you're going to go for a person with money so they can spoil you. So let's go for a penthouse suite in the centre of the city or something.

And if they refuse, just make sure that you cry your fucken eyes out until you get yourself a mansion in the hills.

If you want to take my amazing advice about coming to a compromise when it comes to moving halfway from each other's families, why not just say 'HA, Fuck it' and move to the Maldives. I mean, they have turtles and sunshine, for fuck sake. What more can you fucken ask for? Why would you want to see your parents anyway? It's not like they fucken love you or anything, you piece of shit.

'WHEN IT COMES TO MOVING HALFWAY FROM EACH OTHER'S FAMILIES, WHY NOT JUST SAY 'HA, FUCK IT' AND MOVE TO THE MALDIVES.'

CIAN v EMILY

EMILY!!! HOW MANY FUCKING TIMES DO I NEED
TO TELL YOU, STOP INSULTING THE READERS!

...DON'T YOU EVER TALK TO ME LIKE THAT AGAIN!

LIKE WHAT?! I'M JUST TRYING TO GET THIS INTO
YOUR FUCKING EMPTY HEAD OF YOURS WHERE A
BRAIN SHOULD BE! BUT IT OBVIOUSLY FUCKED OFF.
IN THE PROCESS OF YOUR BIRTH DEVELOPMENT.

Y'KNOW THE WAY THAT YOU WAKE UP SOMETIMES AND
I'M STANDING OVER YOU WHILE STARING QUIETLY?

YEAH?

EVERY TIME I'M DOING THAT, I'M THINKING HOW
MANY SECONDS IT WOULD TAKE TO SMOTHER YOU
SO I CAN HAVE SOME PEACE AROUND HERE.

EMILY, WHAT THE FUCK?

WHAT? JUST SAY SORRY AND I WON'T
SMOTHER YOU WHILE YOU'RE SLEEPING.

OKAY... I'M SORRY?!

THERE'S A GOOD BOY, NOW GO MAKE ME SOME SNACKS.

THE REAL STORY

So as I've mentioned 6,313 times, Emily and I lived over two hours away from each other, which was a bit of a fucking bitch when you think about it. Get a taxi to the bus station, wait 35 minutes to board the bus. Drive two and a half hours to Emily's house on the most boring fucking route you can imagine. It's literally all just fields and then random-ass towns in the middle of fucking nowhere that have only a post office and five bars, typical fucking Ireland. When I arrived, I then got a taxi from the station to her home. With two taxis and a bus ticket, each time I went to see Emily it would cost me €50 up and €50 down, which is about the same in dollars and pounds. So as you can imagine,

it was pretty fucking annoying. Emily somehow ended up sleeping in my house one night and never ended up leaving. My mother kind of just assumed that Emily moved in and took her under her wing like any mother would. Ahhh bless my mother. She's amazing. Anyway, both of us were hesitant to move into our own home at first but the endless months of living in my tiny room together got the better of us. We ended up moving into a penthouse apartment, because hey? Why the fuck not? Emily took the plunge and left everything behind in Waterford to start her new chapter in Cork with me. She's not complaining two years on so I think that we're okay!

WHEN YOU DECIDE TO DECORATE THE HOUSE...

Once of the most important things that's involved with moving into a house is decorating the fucking thing. I think when people first get a house, they don't realise how much bullshit, money and effort goes into it.

If you're renting, a lot of houses come already furnished (in Ireland they do, anyway). But if you're looking to redo the entire home both inside and out, I'll try my best to help you out with my decorating guru skills.

First and foremost, if your girlfriend wants to be in charge of decorating, just fucking let her. There's nothing more elegant than a woman's taste in curtains and cushions. Decorating can be a lot of fun, especially if you're fun and creative. Being young when decorating your house is more of an advantage. Most young people flick through pictures on Twitter or Instagram to see pictures of 'house goals'. They inspire people in their twenties to become a fucking interior designer out of nowhere! Matte black and cream kitchen? Jesus Christ, that's beautiful. Where the fuck did you see this? Oh, I saw it on a tweet so I copied it.

God bless the Internet.

'IF YOUR GIRLFRIEND WANTS TO BE IN CHARGE OF DECORATING, JUST FUCKING LET HER.'

EMILY'S VERSION

Soon I get to move into my own mansion, which by the way should be fucken soon, AM I RIGHT, CIAN?!? So here are a few tips that I have written up to make your life as princess as possible.

* Step 1: The bedroom must be pink. There's nothing worse than having to walk into a bedroom that's painted in a light cream or magnolia, mainly because it looks like you're going to sleep in a fucking waiting room of a nail salon. Get the fuck outta here with that bitch. Get a very, very, very, very bright pink, the kind of pink that'll give you a minor migraine for four to seven hours. Remember, if it ain't bright it's fucken shite.

* Step 2: The doormat must feature a cute and welcoming quote. For example, my doormat says, 'If you're here to try and sell me shit, you best fuck off to one of the neighbours instead'. Welcoming, right? Straight to the point and friendly.

* Step 3: Don't be sleazy, get a Jacuzzi. Put a nice 12-seater Jacuzzi wherever you can fit. Even in the centre of the kitchen so when you put the cupboard on the Jacuzzi it will look like a breakfast bar.

CIAN v EMILY

YOU DO KNOW THAT OUR BEDROOM WALLS WILL NEVER BE PINK, YES?

EHHHH, SAYS WHO?!

SAYS ME, EMILY! I'M NOT GOING TO BE SLEEPING IN A PINK ROOM. YOU'RE 21, NOT FUCKING THREE MONTHS OLD.

OKAY, WELL, WHAT FUCKING COLOUR WOULD YOU LIKE?

MAYBE A NICE AUBERGINE WITH THE BACK WALLS PAINTED VANILLA.

WHY THE FUCK WOULD YOU PAINT OUR WALLS WITH FOOD?

FOOD? THEY'RE COLOURS!

NO, THEY'RE NOT, CIAN. VANILLA IS AN ICE CREAM AND AN AUBERGINE IS THAT VEGETABLE THAT LOOKS LIKE A WILLY.

AUBERGINE IS A SHADE OF PURPLE AND VANILLA IS A SHADE OF CREAM, BABE.

OH. WELL, WHY DIDN'T YOU FUCKING SAY SO? CAN'T YOU JUST SAY PURPLE AND CREAM, YOU FANCY FUCKING PRICK?

THE REAL STORY

So Emily and I can't decorate our home just yet. We're only renting currently and the place was already decorated and, to be fair, whoever decorated it has amazing taste. We were fucking delighted walking into this place cos it looked like something out of a fancy hotel!

Our home has a red, black and cream theme to it. It's cosy as fuck.

We are in the process of buying a home and I think Emily and I are on the same page when it comes to the 'theme' of our future home.

We have a few rules.

We are going to be going for matte black and cream with fucking everything! Imagine this shit now: a matte black kitchen with cream walls and cream tiles. A grey suede couch with a dark mahogany coffee table with red coasters. Oh, Jesus, I'm getting all excited with the thought of it.

If you decorate your bathrooms and kitchen similar, and your living room with your bedroom, you're sorted! Maybe have black and cream for the main colours. Then for each room have a different sub colour like red, turquoise, lime green, orange, etc. for the cushions/curtains/ornaments.

Fucking hell I should have gone into the interior design business.

WHEN YOU HAVE YOUR FIRST NIGHT TOGETHER IN THE HOUSE...

CIAN'S VERSION

This really kind of comes down to if you have furniture in the house or not. Some people spend their first night in their new home lying on a blanket on the floor watching a DVD on the laptop in the centre of the living room.

If your home is already furnished well congratu-fucking-lations. You can just go straight to bed and not have a single fuck to give about anything. So bravo for that, but even though you have all the furniture you could possibly need, you still might just sit there and think, 'What the fuck do I do now?'

Some couples are simple and treat it like any other night. Others might Christen the new home by doing naughty things in every room in the house. Whatever you're into, I guess. My advice in one sentence: you can never beat a good Chinese takeaway with a movie and blankets.

EMILY'S VERSION

Okay, bitches, let's get straight to the fucking point. You've just placed your deposit and the keys have been handed over to you. You've promised the landlord that you'll take good care of their house but as soon as they leave, BOOM motherfucker, it's time to send a text to your WhatsApp group chat to all the girls, we're talking Brandeen, Shaniqua, Daisy-Paloopa, Chrisyshonbonaouiqua, Shon Bon Bon Lagon, Imerialda and Grace. Tell your whole group to get their shit together and gather all of the essentials: vodka, gin, rum, selfie stick, ring light, Anastasia Beverly Hills contour kit, whisky, ice cream, Bridget Jones's Diary on Blu-ray and, of course, pizza. Y'all better not have any vegetarians in your group cos there's nothing worse than having a parsnip lover in the vicinity. Makes you feel all awkward and shit for eating a pig with some cheese and tomato sauce on some dough.

If you have a boyfriend just send him to a different room so you can gossip about him and judge his flaws and make sure that he's the compatible match and will guarantee a rich and luxurious future after a marriage, etc. Y'know, nothing too fancy. You know yourself. Ah ha.

CIAN v EMILY

Cian

Emily, where are you?

Emily

I'm just writing the stuff again, babe.

Cian

What stuff?

Emily

That shitty article you make me write on every fucken page.

Cian

Ohhh ha ha, what did you write about? I trust it was good?

Emily

Ah yeah, it was just about what to do on the first night you move into your home.

Cian

Ahhh yeah, let me guess. You suggested Chinese too?

Emily

Ehmmmmm.... yeah, sure... ha.

THE REAL STORY

The first night Emily and I stayed in our home, we had a few little events occur on the day. Due to our hectic and dramatic lifestyle (sarcasm) we had my mother and her darling partner, Barry, come over, accompanied by my sister. Y'see, getting your own place to stay is a big thing, especially if you're a mother and your child gets their first place, it's an emotional rollercoaster for them. When I told my mother that Emily and I were moving out she started crying hysterically. My poor mom is just an emotional wreck, bless her cotton socks.

So we had them over for the usual tea, coffee and pastry cakes and tours of the house. After that was done, my 'friend' Chris came over and we played Xbox for a little bit, then he fucked off and never returned ever again. When we were finally alone, Emily and I got a big dirty pizza. It was bigger than your fucking head, man. Imagine having the biggest head in the world and still having a pizza bigger than your head. Dude, that must be fucking embarrassing. Once our food was done we both developed food babies and passed out in bed from the amount of carbs we consumed.

WHEN YOU HAVE TO VISIT PARENTS...
CIAN'S VERSION

Remember, people, there's nothing more terrifying that I can think of than drifting away from your parents due to sheer laziness to visit them.

Long distance makes things a little shittier because if you want to see your parents on a frequent basis, financially it'll hurt you a little. Even if it's a five-euro bus ticket, it will all add up throughout the year! I know that it's worth it and you'd spend all your money just to see your parents, but I'm sure there are easier things.

It's also a lovely thing to invite your parents around and cook them dinner. There's nothing more satisfying than spoiling your mother with a home-cooked dinner. I'm sure it's the least you can do, I mean, I'm sure she cooked thousands of meals for you! Give the love back, mannnnn!

If you're missing home, a 30-minute catch-up phone call can sort you right out. My mother calls me every day for 30 minutes and I look forward to them every time. It's just lovely to sit down and listen to her voice. It's calming and soothing.

Also, if you're going to be visiting home, travel less but stay for longer, rather than travelling once a week and staying for only the weekend. Go spend a few days at home. I'm sure your partner can fuck off if they have a problem with it.

'IF YOU'RE MISSING HOME, A 30-MINUTE CATCH-UP PHONE CALL CAN SORT YOU RIGHT OUT.'

EMILY'S VERSION

Since my parents don't exist as I'm just a mere product of a creative mind, I'm going to talk about Cian's dipshit mother, Liz...

Liz is a feisty one, she loves to express her useless opinion like, 'Oh Emily, you shouldn't be buying 24-inch pizzas for yourself' blah blah blah, fuck off you wicked witch.

I try my best to not visit Cian's mother as all she does is stare at my belly rolls and look at my double chins like I'm some type of blubber alien. Fucking bullshit if you ask me.

Cian can be pretty annoying about it too as he gets all defensive saying I never show effort in the relationship. He'd be fucking lost if he didn't get to squeeze my booty at night, so fuck the ungrateful fuck.

LIZ v EMILY

LIZ: HI, EMILY, HOW ARE YOU?

EMILY: OH SHIT. HI, MOMMA TWOMEY, HOW ARE YOU?

LIZ: I'M FINE. LISTEN, I WAS WONDERING, WOULD YOU LIKE TO START GOING TO THE GYM WITH LINDA AND ME?

EMILY: EH... WHY?

LIZ: BECAUSE IT'S GOOD TO GET OUT OF THE HOUSE, DARLING. THERE'S NO NEED TO GET DEFENSIVE.

EMILY: I AIN'T GETTING DEFENSIVE AT ALL, YOU DUSTY OLD FART. YOU'RE CALLING ME FAT BY ASKING ME TO THE GYM.

LIZ: EMILY, IT'S JUST SOME SIMPLE YOGA AND MEDITATION.

EMILY: OKAY, WELL, WHY IS IT AT A FUCKEN GYM, LIZ?! DO YOU ALSO GO TO GET FOOD IN A FUCKING HOSPITAL, YOU FREAKY BITCH?

LIZ: I DON'T UNDERSTAND, EMILY, TALK SOON. SAY HELLO TO MY DARLING SON XXXXX

EMILY: YEAH, WHATEVER BITCH. SEE YA XXX

THE REAL STORY

So Emily and I face a few minor problems when it comes to visiting parents. Emily's are quite far away from us. And my problem is my dad is dead so I can't exactly visit him. I know, that was dreadful, I'm sorry. I like to make sinister and horrible jokes about it, I guess it's how I grieve.

Since I moved out I visit my mom at least once a week. I think it brought us much closer. She rings me every day and I love talking nonsense to her. We could be talking about how there's a sale in Tesco on parsnips and carrots and we'd talk for 20 minutes about vegetables and still love the conversation. That's what I love about my mom, she's also a best friend to me.

We visit Emily's parents as much as possible. We usually go down together in my car and stay for a few nights. Emily's parents are lovely, they're like a second pair of parents to me, and even though none of them know this, sometimes it's nice to talk to Emily's dad as if he were my dad, updating him on things that I'm excited about and stuff. I tell my dad all these things when I'm lying in bed at night. I'd fucking love for him to see what I've been up to right now.

WHEN YOU HAVE TO TACKLE BEDROOM POLITICS...

Having a couple moving into a home together means they'll be sleeping together in the same bed, which also means that they'll be sharing the bedroom. This includes the wardrobe, the underwear drawer, the bedside tables, the storage boxes in the corners of the room, the en suite if there's one there and so on and so on.

Men are generally basic when it comes to things that are kept in the bedroom. A couple of T-shirts, three pairs of black skinny jeans, seven pairs of underwear and some socks, followed by Lynx deodorant and a cheap Hugo Boss aftershave they purchased out of impulse in the duty free in the airport.

The woman, on the other hand, might have a few more bits and pieces to store in and around the bedroom. This may include 400 dresses (half of them never worn), 250 pairs of blue jeans (all of them identical), make-up (more make-up than your average department store), enough hair

pins to supply a Brazilian village, 500,000 pairs of shoes, which will include sneakers, high heels, wedges, stilettos, boots, sandals, flip-flops, slippers, etc.

It's a simple thing: only keep what you fucking need. Whatever you don't need or wear should be stored away in a storage room or attic/loft. There's nothing more frustrating than having clutter in your home. It'll start a fuck-ton of frustrating and unnecessary arguments. You'll just get pissed off for no reason. No one likes to wake up in a fucking dump, so keep it clean, open and vanilla-scented. Oh yeah, baby.

EMILY'S VERSION

There's something that just hugely fascinates me with the male brain. I mean, for some reason they think that they're fucken entitled to claim a certain section of the wardrobe. They clearly don't fucken realise that when they signed up for the relationship they agreed to sacrifice their free time hanging out with the boys, visiting their mothers, laughing or smiling at other women, contacting a woman in general and, most importantly, storage in their own fucken house.

I mean, I have 36 denim jackets that need to be hung up because getting denim wrinkled is like getting dirt in your glass of wine. You can try all you want, but if you want that motherfucker out of your glass, you'd best fucken have the patience of a saint.

Take my advice, ladies, make a little box for him to put his useless shit it. Be nice and make it as large as a shoe box. Plenty of room to store all his stuff while we can have the entire wardrobe, six drawers, three large chests and, of course, the 14-drawer storage unit in the bathroom. Tee-hee, am I fucken evil? Cos I ain't even mad, bitches.

CIAN v EMILY

HEY, BABE, WHEN ARE YOU HOME?

> I'M JUST OUT HAVING SOME MOCKTAILS WITH THE GIRLS. WHY?

AHH, I'M JUST LOOKING FOR MY UNDERWEAR.

> WHICH ONE? YOU HAVE SIX PAIRS. HOW DID YOU LOSE ONE?

I DON'T KNOW, I TOOK IT OFF IN MY SLEEP COS I WAS ALL SWEATY AND SHIT.

> YOU'RE FUCKEN DISGUSTING.

I KNOW... CAN I PUT SOME OF MY T-SHIRTS IN YOUR WARDROBE?

> HAHAHAHAHAHAHAHAHAHAHAHAHA!

WHAT'S SO FUNNY?

> HA HA, NOTHING, I JUST CAN'T BELIEVE YOU THINK I'D FUCKING LET YOU HAVE ACCESS TO THE WARDROBE. GET FUCKED. BE HOME LATER, LOVE YOU, BYEEEE XXXXXX

THE REAL STORY

You know, Emily is a very interesting person. There are multiple things that fascinate me about her. Her personality, her charm, even her giggle. But what fascinates me the most is HOW THE FUCK can someone own so much make-up? I mean, Emily is a hoarder when it comes to make-up. She has fucking years of collected make-up followed by the tons upon tons of free make-up companies send her. You could probably buy a fucking Toyota Yaris with the amount she has. The reason why I'm so frustrated about make-up is because it's scattered over 70 per cent of our room. The windowsills, the en suite, the drawers, in my underwear drawer, even in my fucking pillowcases. And another thing is the wardrobe. I shit you not, people, there is a wardrobe in our room and it's pretty decent. It could accommodate two people with ease to store all of their clothes and shoes. But Emily has the entire wardrobe FULL of jackets. Whether it be denim, tweed, trench coats, leather jackets, bomber jackets, you name it, she fucking has it.

I'm very much tempted to secretly sell all of her things in a car boot sale so I can gather enough cash to fly fucking far away so I can have a wardrobe to myself in peace.

WHEN YOU HAVE TO DO THE JOBS AROUND THE HOUSE...

I don't care what anybody says, there needs to be a team effort when it comes to cleaning the house.

There's nothing more frustrating than having to constantly clean up after someone else. Start off with the old fridge whiteboard. It's the most useful thing in the world. Could be for reminders for shit you don't want to go to. It could be a place to draw a giant penis, if that's your liking. More importantly, it's a good place to write up a to-do list. Have shit to do for you and have shit to do for your partner. Trust me when I say this, a clean house is so fucking good for a relationship. It can literally ruin someone's day having a messy kitchen, then they take it out on their partner. So clean as you go! Vacuum, dust, mop, etc. Consistency is key. If you ate your dinner you'd better fucking go clean the plate straight afterwards, you inconsistent prick.

Try your best to designate permanent jobs for each person who lives in the house. For example, I am in charge of filling and emptying the dishwasher. I have to make sure that job is done daily and because it's done daily, the kitchen is always clean. That's called winning, ladies and gentlemen.

EMILY'S VERSION

Why do jobs when you can just make your life easier by not doing them? Don't use real plates, just use paper plates and plastic forks so you don't have to clean shit. Just put the plates underneath the couch when you're finished and BOOM! Instant cleanliness! Sometimes when I go for a poo I leave giant skid marks on the toilet. My advice for this is to flush just as the poop is airborne, so when the poo hits the toilet bowl, it won't have any time to sit and rest because it's in the middle of a fucking whirlpool flush. It must have been so scared when it was being flushed, RIP, poo.

Sometimes when I'm clipping my toenails, I notice that my nail clippings get stuck in the carpet, so I have a real simple solution for this. When you're cutting your toenails, make sure you're in someone else's home such as a friend, a family member or, if in an emergency, a complete stranger. By clipping your toenails in someone else's home, it means you don't have to pick the clippings up. Instead they will be like, 'Oh hey, when did I clip my toe nails? Silly ole me', but in reality they're just little ole Emily's.

 # CIAN v EMILY

WHERE THE FUCK ARE YOU?

WHY, BABE? WHAT'S WRONG?

DID YOU GO OVER TO MY
MOTHER'S HOUSE TODAY?

NO, BABE, I DIDN'T, I SWEAR!

YOU'RE FUCKING LYING TO ME, I KNOW YOU ARE!

I'M NOT LYING, CIAN! WHY DO YOU THINK I'M LYING?

BECAUSE WHEN MY MOM CAME HOME AFTER WORK
SHE FOUND TOENAIL CLIPPINGS IN THE BATHROOM,
THE KITCHEN, THE PORCH AND THE GARDEN SHED.
WHAT THE FUCK HAVE YOU BEEN DOING?

OHHHHH, IS THAT ALL? YEAH, BABE,
THE WIND WILL TAKE THEM AWAY, DON'T WORRY.

YOU COVERED MY MOTHER'S HOME IN YOUR
FUCKING REPULSIVE TOENAIL CLIPPINGS.

I'LL COVER IT IN MY OWN SHIT THE NEXT TIME
IF YOU DON'T STOP FUCKING COMPLAINING.

THE REAL STORY

So Emily and I face a few problems in our relationship and to be fair, Emily is completely to blame. I mean, sometimes she is just the messiest fucking cocktail sausage I've ever met. She is fucking dreadful when it comes to how many dishes she gets through each day. I mean plates, glasses, bowls and don't get me fucking started with coffee mugs. There's about seven cups I have to clean up before I head to bed.

Now, to be fair to Emily, she's great with everything else, and I am also to blame as I too have an issue. My issue is refusing to hang up clothes. I'm fucking murder for it. I literally could take off my pants and chuck them so far across the room I could end up forgetting about them for weeks.

I clean the kitchen/living room/balcony. Emily cleans the bathrooms and bedrooms.

Honestly, we both suck at cleaning. I mean we get in more arguments because of a messy house than anything else.

Sure I can give you advice about cleaning but in reality I don't fucking clean myself. Fuck it, just be filthy and embrace it. Who needs basic hygiene and health? Pffffft, fucking wimps.

WHEN YOU NEED SOME PRIVACY IN THE HOUSE...

Privacy? What the fuck is privacy? Are you talking about the thing that entitles you to have your own space without anyone being nosy or curious as to what you're doing? Oh yeah, that doesn't exist when you're in a relationship. Somewhere down the line, whether it be in the first few months of your relationship or on the day of your wedding, you're eventually going to see your partner taking a shit. This is just something you have to accept. If you're going to the toilet, your partner will become impatient and come in to wash their face, brush their teeth and put deodorant on their armpits, all while you're sitting there awkwardly trying not to plop as you're not that comfortable with them yet. You could just cough and hope you time it right with the plunge.

Privacy in a relationship is rare, but it's also something that isn't exactly necessary. I mean, most people should be fairly okay with shitting in front of their partner. And if they're not, don't worry, it takes time. Fucking hell, what the fuck am I writing?

Ugh. Kill me now, Satan.

Your partner knows you just as much as you do. So I don't think they care when they see you shit, so chill out, dude. Let the privacy thing chill and shit away.

(How the fuck is that advice?...... moving on.)

EMILY'S VERSION

Ladies, when it comes to having to go to the bathroom, it's most definitely something that needs to be done ALONE. I don't want my boyfriend to walk in on me changing, he'd faint from the fright, the dipshit.

I firmly believe that privacy should exist with poops, pees, tampon pit stop, doing make-up, watching Fifty Shades of Grey when the girls are over and whenever I have a group call with the girls. If the fucker tries coming near me during these hallowed times, he's best keep his balls away from me because I'd kick him into a different month.

Take my advice, treat your man like a puppy. Tell him where he can piss, where he can eat and where he can sleep. Tell him where he can and cannot go and if he disobeys, he gets a slap on the nose. When he's good, give him a treat like a yoghurt or something. I don't know make something up for fuck sake.

I saw Cian coming slowly towards me like a dog creeping towards food on the floor. I warned him that I'm on the phone to Chrisyshonbonaouiqua and if he disobeyed I'd lock him outside the house. He's been out there ever since and it's pretty cold so hopefully he'll learn.

CIAN v EMILY

Cian

Emily, what are you doing?

Emily

I'm brushing my teeth. Why?

Cian

Because well, clearly I'm, eh, taking a shit.

Emily

Oh. Yes. I can see that actually now that you mention it...

Cian

... yeah...

Emily

Wow, what a beautiful posture you have.

Cian

Emmmm, thank you?

Emily

I'm sorry, babe, I'm just panicking because I've never seen you taking a shit before and I didn't eat today so my blood sugar is low so this is actually making me feel like I'm going to pass out.

Cian

Oh well, shit babe, go lie down.

Emily

I would but I need to wash my face.

Cian

But I'm—

Emily

BUT NOTHING I NEED TO WASH MY FUCKING FACE.

THE REAL STORY

So the first time I realised that I had no privacy was the time I was having a shower and Emily just walked right in and started pissing in the toilet. Not a fucking bother to her, may I add. I just stood there with my hands over my thingymajig asking her what the fuck she was doing. She kind of just sat there on her phone watching a video on YouTube not taking much notice of me. I brushed it off. A few weeks later we were going to bed but I popped in to empty the tank and take a seat on the throne.

Emily walks in and brushes her teeth. This was the point that my comfort zone was truly tested. Going for a poo is the only a time a man can get some peace and tranquility.

THE CIAN AND EMILY Q&A – PART THREE

So we've come to the end of yet another chapter. So let's have a fucking quick question and answer round between myself and my alter ego. Oh, Christ, it couldn't get much worse here, I'm so sorry you wasted your money, you could have got three Jägerbombs for the price of this thing.

HOW LONG DO YOU SPEND ON THE TOILET?

CIAN

Ah well, maybe five minutes max. I just sit there and do my business then I move on with my day.

EMILY

Hmmmmm, maybe I would spend 40 to 45 minutes on the bowl. I mean, sometimes I watch Jeffree Star's videos and some of them are fucken long, so yeah, I don't move until I'm finished watching the video. Usually my legs don't work for a few minutes afterwards but it's worth it.

DO YOU THINK PRIVACY EXISTS IN YOUR RELATIONSHIP?

CIAN

I mean, no, not really. Emily constantly comes in while I'm doing something in private like using the toilet or shower.

EMILY

Yeah, Cian usually leaves me alone when I poop. He always says that my poo is 'so smelly it burns my nose cartilage', but I know he's just being polite and respecting my privacy. Aww, bless him.

DO YOU GUYS EVER SHOWER TOGETHER?

CIAN

No, there was this one time we had to because we had limited hot water, Emily kept complaining.

EMILY

No, not really, except that one time Cian had his willy flopping around for the entire fucking thing. I mean, I had my bathing suit on and swimming cap, but Cian had everything off. It was disgusting. I even had my verruca socks on.

IS IT DISRESPECTFUL TO INVADE SOMEONE'S PRIVACY?

CIAN

Absolutely. I find it to be a very insensitive thing. Horrible.

EMILY

Is privacy invasion disrespectful? No, bitch...

PART 4
THE FUTURE

WHEN YOU DECIDE TO BUY A HOUSE...

CIAN'S VERSION

Buying a house is not something that should be rushed into. There's a shit-ton of planning when it comes to getting yourself a place to settle down. Let's talk about finance. How much can you afford? Of course you want a seven-bedroom mansion with a pool and tennis court and shit with a motherfucking treehouse for the kids. You'd love to fucking get that! Who wouldn't? But there's always that little problem: if you want all that shit, that's gonna cost you quite a lot of cash dolla, son.

Even if you can afford it, you need to remember that it doesn't include all of the bills. You'll notice that heating a house costs more than a fucking rare diamond. What makes matters worse is decorating it: paint seems to cost more than the house itself.

If you're 100 per cent sure that both you and your partner are ready to make a huge financial commitment together, you'd best just fucking go for it then.

Have patience with your house and don't rush into anything. Explore as many options as possible and always ask for second opinions from a few family members. You could also save your money and just buy a tent and pitch it in the centre of a roundabout. It's up to you, I'm sure you don't need to be listening to me chatting bullshit about buying a house. What am I, a financial advisor?

EMILY'S VERSION

You're going to want to start off small, aren't you? No! No, you're fucken not. If you want to move in to a house with your hubby, I think it's time you just lower your expectations and settle for a princess castle, sure a €25 million mansion would be nice, but go easy on yourself and spend just a few million. I know that everyone here reading this book can afford that anyway as poor peasants can't relate to me. Only rich bitches understand my vibes, you feel me?

Let's think of a scenario here, when you wake up in the morning in your new home. Do you want to wake up to a smelly shithole or do you want to wake up in a Bel Air mansion with a butler and shit? Well, if you want it, you'd best start selling your clothes on Depop for some extra bits of cash dolla or you can do what I do and that is make my boyfriend, Cian, pay for it. Just give him the sad eyes — works all the time. I promise.

shop online
at selfridges.com

CIAN v EMILY

Emily

> Hey, sweetie.

Cian

> Hey, babe, what's up?

Emily

> Let's do something fun!

Cian

> Ah, like what?

Emily

> You should go to the bank and get a mortgage right now.

Cian

> Emily, what the fuck are you talking about?

Emily

> You heard me, dipshit. I'm sick of living in this crusty-ass house.

Cian

> Emily, we live in a nice modern apartment, what the fuck are you talking about?

Emily

> I'm talking about me being single and ready to fucking mingle if you don't buy me that house up on the hill with the built-in beauty spa.

Cian

> Get fucked, Emily.

Emily

> Fine, I fucking will, with some rich asshole who'll buy me a house. See ya!

THE REAL STORY

It's time for Emily and I to buy an actual home because once you get yourself a home that's yours, you're sorted for life. If all goes to shit with the videos, at least I'll have a home to live in! So yeah, we're in the process of looking for a place to call our home now, and yes, I am trying to get a big snobby-ass house. Something DJ Khaled would live in, do yoga in and shit in the garden, while Emily gets a massage by our future assistant, Ronald. He's going to do our laundry too and prepare French toast with avocado.

WHEN YOU START TALKING ABOUT CHILDREN... CIAN'S VERSION

Now, let's get this out of the way. Let's all agree that I am in no fucking way qualified to tell someone whether or not to have children. Imagine someone reading this and I told them that children are the spawns of Satan. The poor person would be scarred for life. But hey, you bought the book, you get my opinion. That's how it works.

I think you should most certainly enjoy your twenties with only a few minor responsibilities and commitments. I mean, imagine wanting to go for a date somewhere and BOOM! You have no one to mind the kid, ah fuck. What if you want to fuck off to Las Vegas for a weekend? Ha ha, hell naw, you ain't going nowhere, sweetie, cos your motherfucking son has a clarinet recital this fucking Sunday.

It's all down to the individual, isn't it? If you're 20 or fucking 38, have yourself a miniature you running around whenever the fuck you want. So long as it doesn't go near me. I'm kidding, Jesus, don't give this book a bad review for fuck sake. If I'm being serious though, make sure you're ready, financially stable and prepared to never have a lie in ever again.

EMILY'S VERSION

The thought of sitting on a bed screaming until I'm hoarse while grabbing on to Cian's hand like it's the only thing preventing me from fucking myself out of the hospital bed doesn't exactly turn me on. Fucking ew, no thank you, bitch, you can keep it, name it something cute and put up Instagram pictures of it. You can thank me later.

My advice, ladies, just don't do the nasty shit with your boyfriend. I mean, if you're that desperate just hold his hand or something. It's safer than having a little dickhead growing inside of you.

One time my mom (who doesn't actually exist) came up to me and said, 'You better make me a grandmother before I'm 40.'

She wasn't very nice, but that's mothers for you, right?

If you think you're big and bold enough to have a child, well good for fucking you! I'll just raise a few puppies first before I think about shitting out a child.

CIAN v EMILY

BABE?

WHAT?

I HAVE SOME NEWS FOR YOU.

WHAT IS IT, BABE?

WELL, I TOOK A PREGNANCY TEST

OH MY GOD. OKAY. WHAT DID IT SAY?

IT SAID NOTHING, REALLY, SO I GUESS IT'S OKAY.

WHAT THE FUCK DO YOU MEAN IT SAID
NOTHING REALLY? WHAT DID IT SAY?

IT HAS TWO LINES ON IT.

AND WHAT DOES THAT MEAN?

IT SAYS ON THE BOX THAT
IT MEANS I'M PREGNANT.

OH MY... OH MY GOD, EMILY. EMILY, WHAT THE FUCK?!

WHOA, CIAN, WHY THE FUCK
ARE YOU FREAKING OUT?

BECAUSE YOU'RE FUCKING PREGNANT, EMILY!
HOW IS THIS NOT SCARING YOU? WE'RE ONLY 22!

WAIT, I'M PREGNANT? DOES THIS MEAN I CAN
EAT MORE FOOD SO I CAN, Y'KNOW, NURTURE
THE BABY WITH CHEESEBURGERS AND SHIT?

I'M GOING TO PASS OUT.

WELL MAKE SURE YOU CLEAN UP AFTER YOURSELF.

THE REAL STORY

Honestly, I just don't want kids right now. For sure, down the line I hope that Emily and I will have two beautiful children one day. But let me stress, that's not until I'm a little older. After all, I'm a child myself. I can't raise myself out of bed most mornings, let alone raise a fucking child.

Emily and I have already had this discussion. We want two kids, a boy and a girl, named Hudson and Sadie.

The reason I want my son to be named Hudson is that you can't be named Hudson Twomey and not end up being a cool-ass dude. You have no choice but to be a slick dude with the swagger of a Brooklyn b-boy. Okay maybe not that cool but you get me.

Our first child, though, will be a dog. That'll be a good way to see what it's like to clean up shit and piss every eight seconds of your life.

WHEN YOU HAVE TO START THINKING ABOUT WHERE TO LIVE...

CIAN'S VERSION

Okay, so putting the massive amount of stress of moving to one side, before you move into a home have a think about where the fuck you are going to move to.

For me personally, I like to be out in the middle of nowhere but still relatively close to things such as supermarkets and shit. If you have a child, or are planning to have a child, you're going to have to think ahead about where you want them to grow up and where they're going to go to school.

Some people like living in estates, some people like living in the city. Others like living in quiet little suburbs. Whatever kind of place you'd like to live, you should always do a little bit of research. The last thing you want is to move into somewhere that has fucking riots every Friday night. Get yourselves one of them nice neighbourhoods where you pay the nice lady to cut your grass every month in the summer.

I may sound like a diva here, but my ideal place would be up a nice country back road. Big gates with a fancy code to open it which leads to a drive up to my home with a big garden for my 60 dogs I plan to raise and live with. Can you imagine having 60 golden retrievers in your garden? Oh, God, a boy can fucking dream, can't he?

EMILY'S VERSION

You're going to need to fucking plan this shit very carefully, okay? Get your notepads out and jot this down. Is your home near a tanning salon, a nail salon, a McDonald's, a cinema, an arcade with unicorn rides, a crèche to put your dipshit kid in so you don't have to worry about it during the day? If you're close to all of them, you're good to fucken go.

I plan to have a grumble of pugs surrounding the perimeter of my home. About 15 will do. They will be a fence to prevent any intruders from coming onto the property. They're vicious little shits when they want to be.

It's also necessary to have a separate building to the house on the property. You could put some beanbags in there so whenever you argue with your boyfriend you can send him to the disappointed house in the back garden where he can sit and reflect on how much of an asshole he is. Trust me, ladies, you gotta be prepared for this kind of shit.

CIAN v EMILY

Emily

Y'know when we move into our home?

Cian

Yeah?

Emily

Can we live near a pony farm?

Cian

Why?

Emily

Because.

Cian

Because what?

Emily

Because ponies.

Cian

Oh, Emily, will you just fuck off and stop making everything about yourself.

Emily

I'm not, I'm just saying ponies are a relative to the unicorn and I find that very fascinating, which is why I want to live close to the magical creatures.

Cian

Just give up, babe.

Emily

I'll give up after I have my fucking ponies.

THE REAL STORY

Emily and I keep on failing to think about the future, we keep forgetting to talk about when we have children and dogs and other shit, like where to raise our kids and what school to go to and what kind of friends they should have and if there's a child abduction history in the town. I do realise that part was slightly insensitive but I'm usually pretty calm, so give me a break.

The good thing about Emily is she has the exact same style and taste as I do. We both want a house with a matte black door and we both want a place that looks shitty on the outside but amazing on the inside. You gotta fool the haters, you see, haters are my motivators after all. Pffft, no one gets haters. People are entitled to hate you, dipshits. Go fuck yourself.

Please don't throw the book away I promise it's nearly over, you can go soon!

WHEN YOU START LOOKING FOR A PET... CIAN'S VERSION

Getting a pet together is most definitely a big deal. Think about it, you're going to team up with your partner and look after an animal until the day it dies. Let's use dogs for an example, mainly because dogs are the greatest things that have ever graced this planet. I fucking love dogs, man. I mean, if there was a puppy and its careless owner drowning in a lake, I would save the puppy first then go back to the asshole who got too close to the water. Sometimes humans don't deserve dogs.

Anyway, sorry I'm going so off topic. If you're living in rented accommodation, you need to find out if pets are permitted in the home. There's nothing worse than getting a dog, only to hear that your little puppy can't stay. So you either move into a place that allows pets or you give your puppy to a new home. If that was me I'd have snot bubbles and red cheeks for weeks from the heartbreak.

If you want a pet, be ready to commit to playing with them, walking them daily, feeding them, training them, raising them, etc. It's like having a newborn baby only the newborn baby won't scream when you leave it in the other room while shitting all over the cream carpets. Or maybe it will… I'm sure that's probably happened before, I mean it sounds pretty possible.

Bentley   FOLLOW   ...

GO F*CK YOURSELF CIAN

♥ 2571 likes
Bentley #dog #fuckingdog #petstragram #fuckCian

EMILY'S VERSION

So you wanna get yourself a pet, right? Okay cool. First you need to make sure you're either unemployed or you work from home because you're going to need to attend to the fucker for every minute of the day. Whether it's a puppy, a kitten or a 12-foot majestic unicorn, you're going to need to fucken commit to the bitch. If they shit all over your carpet or eat your make-up, hit them on the nose with a make-up brush, that'll teach the little prick for trying to ruin your prestigious collection of beauty products.

Make sure you make an Instagram for the pet. I mean what other reason would you want the smelly thing anyway? Get thousands of followers and exploit your furry friend by doing brand deals for fucking dog toy companies. Of course that's going to work.

'MAKE SURE YOU MAKE AN INSTAGRAM FOR THE PET. I MEAN WHAT OTHER REASON WOULD YOU WANT THE SMELLY THING ANYWAY?'

CIAN v EMILY

Emily

Do you like the name Bentley?

Cian

I guess it's nice, yeah, why??

Emily

Because that's what I'm naming our puppy.

Cian

Puppy? What fucking puppy?

Emily

Oh yeah, I forget to mention I'm currently in a room waiting for a man to give me one of his puppies.

Cian

Emily, what the absolute fuck?!? Please tell me you're kidding.

Emily

Lol, nah babe, I'm only joking.

Cian

Okay, thank God. I thought I was going to have to break up with you there, lol.

Emily

...

Cian

Hello?

Emily

Myself and Bentley will be home shortly, boil the kettle.

THE REAL STORY

This part of the book has a sad ending, for when I was planning a birthday surprise for Emily, I asked my letting agent about pets and was told that there are no dogs allowed. GOD FUCKING DAMN IT! I had it all planned out. I was going to come home with a puppy and leave it in Emily's arms so she could hyperventilate and pass out from the sheer awe and cuteness of having a nine-week-old puppy chilling on your lap. Have you ever seen a puppy at nine weeks old? It's fucking adorable, just trust me; google it if you don't believe me.

But anyway, once she said no, my heart shattered into 900 pieces. I was so fucking ready to have a little dipshit running around pissing all over the kitchen and biting the curtains until I have to replace them.

I would have got a long-haired miniature dachshund. He's out there somewhere, running on a beach without me. Oh, for fuck sake I'm feeling all emotional now. But hey, it's okay! When the time is right it'll happen. Hopefully Emily and I will be able to buy a home and have 6009 dogs running around in every possible room in the house. Fuck yeah, that's the dream, baby.

WHEN YOU START TALKING ABOUT MARRIAGE... CIAN'S VERSION

Ah marriage, the scariest word in all of the land. Where the falling brothers lie in silence as they listen to their fiancée talking about whether they want their bridesmaid dresses to be royal blue or aqua blue. Just pick a fucking colour, dickhead, for fuck sake.

Marriage is likely to be the biggest thing of your life. The traditional goal is to be healthy, have a good job, have a nice house with kids and be FUCKING MARRIED!

Lots of people are afraid of getting married and, quite frankly, I don't blame them! Shit man, I don't know if I'll still like lasagne in 40 years. I mean, what if I get sick shit of Emily and leave her to become a monk? To be fair, that's rather unlikely. I'd become an NFL player instead.

What pisses me off with marriage is when people treat it like it's a fucking joke. Some pair of fucking twats get married and divorced on the same day like how the fuck could your day have gotten so miserable. Don't rush marriage and if you're pressuring your partner then you should go fuck yourself you piece of shit.

I'm just kidding, please forgive me, but hey! If the shoe fits... *, sips on cup of tea*.

'LOTS OF PEOPLE ARE AFRAID OF GETTING MARRIED AND, QUITE FRANKLY, I DON'T BLAME THEM! SHIT MAN, I DON'T KNOW IF I'LL STILL LIKE LASAGNE IN 40 YEARS.'

'WILL YOU EVER JUST FUCKING MARRY ME, CIAN. I'M GETTING BEYOND BORED AT THIS STAGE.'

EMILY'S VERSION

I've been sitting here for two years now, hoping that one day Cian is going to grow a pair of balls and marry my hot ass. But sadly, the ungrateful asshole still remains seated in his gaming chair eating popcorn and playing on the Xbox, while I'm in the background planning my marriage and planning on how I can divorce Cian and take half of his shit. I'm remaining optimistic about this. Christmas is coming up so hopefully he'll get the idea. I know that I asked him for a new Range Rover but he's smart enough to know that it's just a code word for marrying me. Bless him, he's so naive, the little prick.

Ladies, if you want your man to marry you, just give him a few subtle hints, such as a sticky note on the fridge or maybe even a hot air balloon to land in your back garden with a sign on it saying, 'Will you ever just fucking marry me, Cian. I'm getting beyond bored at this stage.'

That usually works, but if it sadly doesn't, just channel your inner Beyoncé and do the single ladies dance to him. Then leave the prick.

 # CIAN v EMILY

EMILY TWOMEY HAS A NICE RING TO IT, DOESN'T IT?

YEAH, IT'S FINE. WHY ARE YOU SAYING THAT?

SOLVE THE PUZZLE:
W_L_ Y_ _ M_RRY _ E?

WILL YOU MARRY ME?

OMG, CIAN, THIS IS SO
SUDDEN. I WOULD LOVE TO.

WAIT, WHAT THE FUCK? NO,
EMILY, YOU CAN'T JUST DO THAT.

WELL, I JUST DID, AND I SCREENSHOTTED
IT AND SENT IT TO THE GIRLS IN
THE GROUP CHAT SO YOU CAN PRETTY
MUCH SAY IT'S OFFICIAL. CONGRATS ON
GETTING ENGAGED TO ME, DICKHEAD. XXX

THE REAL STORY

So many fucking people ask me, 'Oh when are you going to marry Emily' or, 'You should definitely marry Emily'. Okay, cool, that's nice. I didn't fucking ask for your input though, did I, you dickhead!

Since starting the videos, everyone always asks me whether I want to marry Emily or not. Of course I do, she wouldn't be my girlfriend otherwise. What's the point of having a temporary girlfriend?

Having a girlfriend is just the first stage of having a wife.

Why make a shit-ton of memories and make huge impacts on each other's lives then say, 'Okay, cool, that was fun, see you later, motherfucker.'

I'm here to swim lengths, I'm not here for a quick dip.

'HAVING A GIRLFRIEND IS JUST THE FIRST STAGE OF HAVING A WIFE.'

WHEN YOU THINK ABOUT PROPOSING... CIAN'S VERSION

Gentlemen, this advice is for you and you only, unless of course you're a woman who wants to propose. So technically I should just say that this advice is for anyone who wants to propose. Yeah let's go with that.

I personally have no experience in proposing so my suggested actions may or may not work. So if you're after proposing and your partner says no, please don't fucking blame me, okay? But if it works out you need to thank me and send me flowers and pay for my future mortgage. Thank you so much, awww you're so kind.

If you have a partner who loves you for you, you're off to an advantage. Of course, if your partner doesn't love you for you then you've got yourself an issue and should work on that before you get down on one knee.

I want you to genuinely sit down and think, 'What's the best way to propose to my partner?'

We'll get the obvious thing out of the way: you can't buy love and affection. So there's no point renting out an entire football stadium that spells

'Stacey, will you marry me' spread across the field with words made out of diamond rings. Yeah, that's cool, you just spent 3.8 billion dollars but your new fiancée is only with you because you got yourself a fat-ass wallet.

If you're wanting to propose, you'd best fucking get down on one knee and pour your fucking heart out to them. Grab their hand and give them the most genuine look into their eyes. Genuine romance is the key, make it memorable for them. For it's the most important question they'll ever be asked.

EMILY'S VERSION

Ladies, I have prepared a step-by-step strategy for subliminally convincing your partner to get down on their knee. I like willies, so I am talking about a man proposing to me. If you're a lady and you like lady willies, just translate everything from 'him' to 'her'.

* **Step 1:** Use alphabet fridge magnets to spell out 'When the fuck are you going to marry me?' I personally find this an effective strategy as Cian visits the fridge 30 to 40 times a day; he does love his cheese board.

* **Step 2:** When you're getting funky in the bedroom, instead of saying anything weird and sexy, try saying, 'Oh, future husband' or, 'Oh yeah, I'm your fiancée soon, hopefully please'. He'll never want to leave you again.

* **Step 3:** When it's your turn to make the dinner, try your best to add some hints to his plate of food. Sometimes I like to put a wedding dress on his steak to associate his favourite food with me looking like a steak in a wedding dress. I'm just projecting an image of what he can look forward to on his wedding day. I'll even have garlic butter in my hair because I'm a seasoned little bitch.

CIAN v EMILY

Cian
> Let me ask you something.

Emily
> Oh my fucking God, okay?

Cian
> Well, you know the way that I love you more than anything in this world?

Emily
> Cian, I'm going to shit myself. Just ask me already, you fucking prick.

Cian
> Will you do me the honour of joining me tonight for some pizza?

Emily
> Oh for fuck sake, Cian. I thought you were going to fucking ask me to marry you. You're such a fucking wank stain. I hate you more than I hate your mother. You should go fuck yourself.

Cian
> Babe, I'm so sorry.

Emily
> It's okay. So what time is the pizza cos I could eat a fucking ostrich right now.

THE REAL STORY

Have I ever proposed to somebody? Nope. Have I ever considered proposing to somebody? Nope. Do I plan on proposing to Emily anytime soon? Fuck no.

I find that rushing shit is just messy. Sometimes Emily jokes around with the whole 'Cian, when the fuck are you going to propose to me' and quite frankly, I feel like shitting in her pillowcase every time she does that. I mean, I'm not going to go anywhere, the only difference is you'll have a big fucking ring that I can't afford on your finger.

I'm a young dude, 22 to be exact but probably 23 by the time you're reading this. I don't have to get engaged right now. I know I'll be marrying Emily, but I'm in no rush to pop the question. There's nothing wrong with it, but there's also nothing wrong with not rushing. I've been with Emily for only two years. To put it in comparison to the rest of our lives, two years is nothing. So let's go through some more tough shit and challenges to test how fucking strong we really are. I love Emily to death and I most certainly plan on asking her to marry me. Just not right now. Okay, Emily? You fucking stressful bitch! (I love you.)

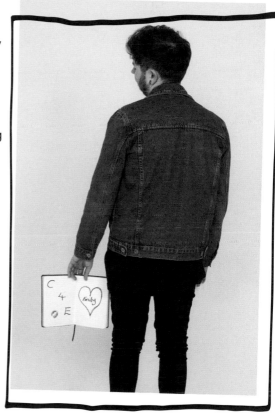

WHEN YOU TALK ABOUT YOUR HONEYMOON... CIAN'S VERSION

So you've proposed, a few months or years pass, and now you are happily married to your partner. Congratulations, you didn't die in the process. Now that you've got through the wedding, it's time to go on a honeymoon. Some people like city breaks, others go back to countries that remind them of a significant time that they shared together, others fuck off to the Bahamas for some sun, sex and coconut cocktails. Whichever you prefer, it's always nice to fuck off with your new wife and not worry about anything in the bullshit real world.

My ideal place would be Amsterdam, and no, it's not because of the legal weed. Ha ha. Yeah... cough... it's most definitely not for the weed, okay? Can I get that into your brains? It is not for the weed, pass the blunt.

I visited Amsterdam with Emily and thought it was just the most beautiful city ever. The streets are nice and narrow, the people friendly and kind. Barely any cars, just a shit-ton of cyclists who don't knock you down. And then there's the weed cafes, oh wait, shit. Never mind, I was joking. Yeah. Please don't tell my mom.

EMILY'S VERSION

There's nothing more exciting than going on your honeymoon. It's just a shame that you have to bring your husband with you because he's just going to try touch your titties the whole time.

I have had my honeymoon planned since I was six years old.

I want to go to the Maldives and swim with dolphins and sea turtles and shit like that. There needs to be multiple locals who will give up their lives to become my full-time servants. I've prepared multiple jobs such as fan-blower, grape-feeder, foot-massager, sun-cream applier, balloon-animal maker, professional complimenter who will provide multiple compliments such as, 'Emily, your bum is so sexy.'

The food will be cooked by my personal chef, named Hanz. The name has to be Hanz or I won't enjoy it. I've seen all this in a vision, FYI. The food needs to be vegan, except if there's chicken or steak. I also will require a man with abs who isn't my husband so I can just stare at him doing some sit-ups on the beach while I eat grapes in the shade under a fucken palm tree. Cian won't know a thing because all he does is nap and when he's not napping he's trying to touch my tits and I feel like castrating him every fucken time.

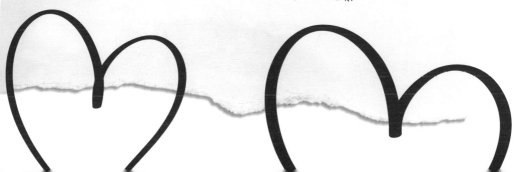

CIAN v EMILY

HELLO, HUSBAND.

WE'RE NOT MARRIED, EMILY.

OH, I KNOW THAT, BUT LET'S DO A
THAT'S SO RAVEN ON IT AND HAVE
A VISION INTO THE FUTURE.

OKAY, AND WHY SHOULD WE DO THAT?

BECAUSE, MOTHERFUCKER, I NEED TO
PREPARE YOU FOR THE INEVITABLE.

HA HA, KEEP UP DOING THIS
AND YOU'LL BE FUCKING SINGLE.

YEAH, WELL, I'LL FUCK OFF TO BALI ON MY OWN AND
FUCK A CUTE LITTLE SURFER WITH ABS AND SHIT.

OKAY, EMILY, AND HOW
WILL YOU GET THERE?

I'LL SELL MY LIPSTICK COLLECTION ON EBAY.

THE REAL STORY

I think when my honeymoon comes, Emily and I will return to a place that we loved. I know I mentioned Amsterdam above, but that's my ideal honeymoon, not Emily's, and to be fair, Emily deserves to go wherever the fuck she wants for our honeymoon. I do believe that Emily wants to go somewhere exotic such as the Maldives, Bali or some other place that costs about €15000 to fly there, lol, fuck my life. Hopefully, Emily's father will be amazing and pay for the entire thing. After all, I did buy him a golf trolley so I'm sure he'll pay

me back with a five-star honeymoon. Thanks, Seamie, you're the best. You sexy silver fox, you.

If my honeymoon consists of not seeing a single person other than Emily for two weeks and spending every day chilling on the beach with nobody else around and drinking Coke from a glass bottle, that'd suit me down to the fucking ground. I'd be a happy little camper if that were to come true. Emily, I am giving hints, yes, go off and get rich, please and thank you.

WHEN YOU THINK ABOUT GETTING OLD...

CIAN'S VERSION

I am a firm believer in 'you're as young as you feel', and to be fair my grandmother Emily (yes, she has the same name as my girlfriend) is in her late seventies but she has a young soul. She always says she can't wait for her 23rd birthday, and to be honest I believe her when she says it.

She lost her husband recently after being with him since she was 17, but she remains as positive as possible, even though we all know she is just completely lost without him. She's an inspiration when it comes to relationships. They were truly in love and they spent every day together from the moment they met on a bus in Cork to when my grandad took his last breath. It's bittersweet, she lost the love of her life but even though he died, the legacy they left lives on. They have seven kids, 14 grandkids and two great-grandkids. They lived a full and happy life together and that's all that matters. That's what actual relationship goals is. Not some shitty wannabes on a beach in Ibiza. I want Emily and me to be like my grandparents. With each other till death do does us part. It's like a movie, isn't it?

Anyway, I'd hate to leave this on a sad note, but I just thought this topic should be left with a little bit of dignified emotion rather than making silly jokes about it. Live your life and love to live! Grow as old as you can and have a fuckload of fun during it. If I'm quite honest it's 3 a.m. in the morning and I'm finally coming to the end of writing my book and it's a little bit emotional so I thought it'd be nice to have a little story time about my grandparents. They were the best couple, good ole Georgie and Emily!

THE CIAN AND EMILY Q&A – PART FOUR

WHEN AND HOW SHOULD I PROPOSE?

CIAN

I think you know when the time is right to propose. You'll either have a moment of realisation during some conversation with your partner and you'll think, 'Oh my God I want to marry this sexy bitch', while others slowly realise they want to marry their partner so they just plan the living shit out of when and how to propose. For example, my cousin Shane got proposed to by his girlfriend. She proposed to him on the 29th of February, which is a leap year. She had to plan the living fuck out of that! Or she just realised that it was cool for a woman to propose on the leap year so she was like 'fuck it he ain't asking me so imma ask him'. I should really just ask them, that'd work a little better.

Usually I feel that girlfriends expect it around anniversaries or Christmas times, maybe even Valentine's Day but they might think that's too predictable. I would personally just catch Emily by surprise and propose to her when she's least expecting it. Not when she's taking-a-shit kind of surprised but maybe during a city-break holiday like Paris or some shit. But again, Paris is too predictable. SO maybe we could try Bosnia and Herzegovina. She wouldn't even know.

As for how to propose, like I said earlier: let your heart do the talking. I know that your heart can't physically talk, but you get where I'm coming from, you fucking smartass. Get down on one knee and ask her as honestly and as passionately as possible, motherfucker. You'd better cry too for extra effect. Women love it when you cry, I've heard it's the key. It's what my grand-uncle William Lover said, and he knew his women. He's responsible for the population of south Ireland. He's not really, in fact he doesn't even exist.

EMILY

You should kinda propose whenever the fuck she says so. I mean I've asked Cian 34 times so far but baby don't you worry, I ain't giving up yet.

I think you need to be 'Facebook official' for at least one month before you consider getting down on your knee and popping the potentially regretful question. Of course Cian is dying to ask me, but I know that he is just spending a super-long time planning how he's going to ask me. I've dropped numerous hints that I want him to descend from a hot air balloon riding a unicorn and wearing a white suit with some pink Gucci flip-flops. Ahhhhh, yeah that's the dream alright baby.

I'VE GOT COLD FEET ON THE MORNING OF MY WEDDING. WHAT SHOULD I DO?

CIAN

Y'know, because these questions are just made up I understand that it's fine, but if someone ever messaged me asking this question, I'd just stare at them in awe. First of all, why the fuck are you messaging me on the day of your wedding? Secondly, why have you got to be such a dickhead that you have second doubts on the day of the wedding. You had five years, nine months, three weeks, six days, 14 hours and 43 minutes to decide whether you wanted to marry your partner or not. How fucking dare you be selfish enough to cancel on the day? You've just permanently shattered your partner's life and publicly embarrassed him or her in front of their entire family. I know I'm sounding a bit harsh but you see this could save somebody soon.

To sound more reasonable and gentle, if you're having doubts about your wedding and you feel pressured to say, 'I do', just sit down with your future husband/wife – maybe bring along the parents – and just talk it out. You never know, everyone could agree and end up rescheduling the wedding to a much later time. Yeah, it was a total waste of money and you lost your deposit, but you also prevented a life-changing catastrophe.

I'm passionate about this topic because whenever I see it in movies or TV shows, it proper pisses me the fuck off because the groom is left there crying, being consoled by their ex-future-in-laws and their best man. It's always heart-breaking seeing a man ruined and shattered by a partner, kind of similar to an elderly person crying. You don't want to see that or there'll be snot bubbles everywhere.

EMILY

What should you do? You should go fuck yourself that's what you should do. What kind of stupid, self-centered, idiotic BITCH would walk away from their favourite booty at the church? Bitch you ain't just getting feelings the day of the church; if you didn't want to marry him, well, you shouldn't have said 'yes' when you saw that big fat diamond ring! Although I, too, would do every single thing that you have done, as I can't resist me a good diamond...

THE CIAN AND EMILY Q&A – PART FOUR

I HATE HIS SURNAME; HELP!

CIAN

If you hate his surname, you should do me a huge favour and get that little hammer there and use it to build a bridge that'll enable you to get the fuck over it. If you love your man, the last thing you should be concerned about it is having to take his surname. That's what people do, they make sacrifices. Emily will be called Emily Twomey, and I think that's weird because I actually like Emily Rochford. Maybe you can keep both names. So we'd be Cian & Emily Rochford-Twomey. It kind of sounds fancier anyway. Hi, I'm Cian Rochford-Twomey, it's a pleasure to meet you *lights Cuban cigar and sips on 24-year-old scotch in a bath robe*.

So yeah, to answer the somewhat complicated question. The worst-case scenario is you just take both names and merge them together.

EMILY

Oh boo fucking hoo someone fetch me a tissue for this picky twat. If I met a real hunk whose name was 'Diego Fartinmapussay' I wouldn't even mind. I mean I do look like an 'Emily Fartinmapussay'. It's a cute name if you pronounce it differently to the spelling. I like to pronounce 'Fartinmapussay' as 'fartile-petit pois' which is French for 'Little Lavender', I think...

If you're worried about his fuckin' surname well you should be grateful that you live a life that contains no real fuckin' worry. You ignorant fucking bitch sweet baby Jesus don't make me get my nails out.

And that my lovely people is the end of my Q&A. I do hope you have enjoyed my words and I'm sorry I couldn't answer more. I'm just so famous that my schedule is too cramped to fit in any more struggles that I don't have to deal with because I have multiple assistants in my life to help me.

ACKNOWLEDGEMENTS

EMILY:

You've built the page with me, you've edited my videos with me, you've filmed everything for me, you've helped me with scripts and ideas when I couldn't focus, you've built and helped me develop the crazy 'Emily' character, who's loved by a shit-tonne of people. You've done too much for me, you've supported me with everything and I wouldn't have any of this cool Internet shit without you. I thank you and I love you. You're the best. (Side note: follow Emily on Instagram: missemilyrochford (haha I gotta get that shoutout in! I always got, you don't worry!))

MOM:

Ahhh, Liz, where do I start with you? Well first I just want to thank you for being so supportive with me and raising me to be the man that I am today. Thank you for keeping me safe throughout the years, thank you for telling me everything was okay when it wasn't, thank you for looking at me with pride and joy and believing that I could do anything I wanted. Thank you for allowing me to drop out of college. Thank you for hugging me anytime I got upset. Thank you for protecting me over the years. Thank you for telling me that people who are nasty are just jealous assholes and eventually I can write about it in a book! (Finally I get to say it!)

You're the best Mom and I hope you're proud. Thank you for being the strongest person and best role model in my life.

REBECCA:

You're the biggest dipshit of a sister ever and you've driven me to tears with stress and you still do to this day, but regardless I just want to say that you've actually helped me a lot. When Dad died I kinda felt responsible to stand and look over you, and thanks to that you've helped me grow independent and mature! Also thanks for understanding Emily and myself when 're grumpy. I love you! You'll get to write a book too soon; have patience!

MY FRIENDS AND FAMILY:

I have too many to name but I just want to thank every single person who's helped me out with everything in both my life and my weird Internet job. I've taken a little piece from everyone in my life and used it to be the best person I can be.

THE PEOPLE WHO GAVE ME SHIT:

I want to thank any fucking dickhead who hates me. Without you I'd be stuck in the mud and I needed something to motivate me to be better each day. I'm reaching my goals and making my momma proud so stick that up your fucking a..........

DAD:

I'm going to keep this short, but I'd especially like to dedicate this book to my father, Paul. If you ask any family member if me and my dad are similar, they'll say that talking to me is like talking to my dad. My dad had his issues and his problems but they were fizzled away by the happy memories I've had growing up. I was lucky enough to have a taste of what it was like to have a father and even though it's now all gone, the memories will never fade.

Thank you for giving me your eyebrows, your humour and your everything else. I am the man I am today because of you and I thank you for it. Hopefully we will meet again and I can fill you in with all this weird shit going on in my life. It's a tiny bit different since you left the world. I will love you forever, Dad.

AFTERWORD
BY MY SISTER, REBECCA

What was it like growing up with my brother before he started creating his videos? Well, Cian was always a character, and like a normal brother and sister we constantly fought, and hell broke loose once or twice. There were a few laughs, a few tears, but at the end of the day he was and still is the person I look up to.

When I was around eight-years-old, Cian used to be in a local Scouts group and he had quite a lot of neckerchiefs. One night, when Cian was babysitting me, he decided to play a prank with the neckerchiefs and it ended in me being tied to the leg of a table in the dark. It also ended up with me in tears. Looking back on that I find it hilarious and I'm sure he would too. My friends ask me what's it like having a 'celebrity' brother; and, you know, it's the same answer every time: 'Meh… yeah it's okay…' or 'Yeah, pffftttt, whatever', but really what I'm thinking is, wow, my brother has millions of followers and that millions of people watch his videos and get entertained by them, which is pretty freaking cool; I mean, wouldn't you like to have a brother who professionally plays the recorder out of his nostrils?

In all seriousness, though, I idolise my brother, not because we have the same sense of humour or because he is paying me for every word in this paragraph, but because he has achieved so much for his age. He has brought Emily into our family (the real Emily) and she treats me like the sister I never had and I'm sure she feels the same way. I look up to Cian and Emily and I am constantly proud of their achievements.